The Gift of Play

The Gift of Play

Why Adult Women Stop Playing And How To Start Again.

Barbara Brannen

Writers Club Press
San Jose New York Lincoln Shanghai

The Gift of Play
Why Adult Women Stop Playing And How To Start Again.

Writers Club Press
an imprint of iUniverse, Inc.

For information address:
iUniverse, Inc.
5220 S. 16th St., Suite 200
Lincoln, NE 68512
www.iuniverse.com

Cover Design by Sherry Moon and Jodie Brown,
Brannen, Barbara, 1949—
the gift of play, why adult women stop playing and how to start again

ISBN: 0-595-23426-7

Printed in the United States of America

To Michael

This book is lovingly dedicated to Michael. Your steadfast support of me in my work has shown no bounds. Your love, and your patience have been a blessing like no other. You have also been my inspiration to find my "Heart Play" by your wonderful example and love of life. I hope you will always know how much I love you and how grateful I am to have you as part of my life.

"We don't stop playing because we grow old, we grow old because we stop playing."

C. Wyatt Runyon

CONTENTS

ACKNOWLEDGEMENTS

There are so many people that helped with this labor of love that it is hard to know the right words to say thank you. First, Hae Won Kwon, a world of gratitude for your marvelous editing. You made my words sing and truly understood my message. There is no doubt in my mind that you are one of the best things that ever happened to this book.

Sherry Moon, your enthusiasm and smile made all your illustrations that much more meaningful. Your persistence to get this formatted and finally delivered kept me from the funny farm in the closing moments. Joe Biene, thank you for being there for me and your warm patience during my frantic moments. Mary Guess, as always, a champion in my moments of need and a blessing in my life.

To my sister Emily, what can I say except you are the best! You shared your stories, helped me remember mine, and never, ever gave up on me. Your enthusiasm for this project was a gift I will always cherish.

To Chris and Pat, thanks for letting me disappear so many times. Thank you for the sacrifices you made so that this dream could become a reality. You have also been an inspiration to me as you play and laugh and love. I am a lucky Mom to have you two guys.

Mom and Dad you have always believed in me from day one and this has been more of an inspiration to do this book than you can imagine. Thank you for the love and the believing.

The characters in this book are compilation characters. What that means is that I have taken pieces of stories and woven them together to create stories. For the wonderful, marvelous, incredible, delightful women who let me pick their brains and their stories I can only say thank you for the bottom of my heart. Cheri L., Ann W., Maureen T., Carol M., Gwen C., Joan R., Diane W., Denny K., Kathy F., Theresa H., Linda S., Kathy O., Pamela B., Diane P., Annie N., . Bronwyn C., Kate R., Lois H., Ann

B., Ruth L., Sheila B., Jim J., Bev O., David G., Joe W., Susan D., Julie A., Marj K., Deb V., Cindy B and Barbara A..

A very loving and special thank you to the WonderWomen in my life who have provided not only love and support, but pulled me off the edge of the cliff many times while writing this book; Jodie Brown, Cheri Knopinski, Emily Hall, Beverly Obenchain, Sally Schweizer and Lynne Zucker. You are my heart.

PROLOGUE

My company, Playmore, came about in 1999 when I realized that life had much more to offer me than I was getting. My life was filled with work, family, community and many other things. While I still enjoyed having fun sometimes, real play seemed frivolous and had no priority in my life. Then I left my job, lost my health, and one of my children became seriously ill. The grave nature of all these things forced me to sit back, look at the horizons of my life and ask the question, "how can things be better?"

This book was written to help women look at play as being as important as anything else in their lives. Why? Because hidden in our play is the real person that we are. When we honor this person, we open our hearts and our minds to all that is important, even sacred, to us. Not what others think is important or fun or playful, but what we truly feel is our play and who we are. For far too long women have taken the high road of responsibility, reliability, accountability, and just plain old-fashioned endurance to keep their worlds running. On occasion they relax, refresh, and re-energize, but usually not well, or often, and not in the form that I call "Heart Play."

"Heart Play" is unique to every human being on earth. It allows you to be totally in the moment, involves no unwelcome work, and comes without responsibility. It creates an ecstasy that may not be apparent to anyone but you. "Heart Play" makes your heart sing and fly free. "Heart Play" changes your perspective and opens your mind. It allows you to see, feel and hear things the way you truly perceive them and not as they are interpreted to you by others in meetings, memos, through the media, in speeches or in signs.

Getting in touch with my "Heart Play" was a long and arduous journey. I had forgotten how to play and what play I liked. I could not find time in my life to play, even when I was unemployed! I doubted my own thoughts about the importance of play. The ability to honor play was absolutely foreign to me. Despite a childhood of play and playfulness, I no longer had the ability as an adult to really feel the same joy that I had felt in childhood play.

In a world that requires work to earn a wage, responsibility to care for families, exercise to maintain our health, prayer and community service, where does play come in? This was the question I needed to explore, and thus my journey began.

Come with me as we listen to my story and those of many others who have taken the leap to find their "Heart Play." Walk back into your childhood and rediscover the joy and wonderment of play. Explore what your own true "Heart Play" might be, and then begin to color your life with it and watch the changes begin. I suggest you read this book, not as a project, but in nibbles and pieces over time. Let the stories here trigger good memories. Let the thoughts here guide you toward discovering your "Heart Play," and then make it an important part of your life.

You deserve every playful moment you can get. You are worth it. Have Fun!

1
Barbara's Story — Where the Book Got Kick-Started

When I started writing about play and came up with the idea for this book, the furthest thing from my mind was to do this chapter. In the process of interviewing people along the way, I kept getting the message to tell my own story. Initially this seemed a little strange, but as I saw myself like everyone else reading this book, the idea eventually took hold.

I grew up in a world full of play. We lived in the country with fields, forest, and streams all around my home. There was one very small grocery store down the highway, my father and uncle's sawmill was just a short few steps from the house, and no other commercial ventures were nearby. The closest town was three miles away, a million miles to a child, so we made our nearby environment, our playground.

In the summer we were up and out the door as quickly as we could manage before too many "chores" showed up for us. We had a swing in the backyard, a sandbox, trees to climb and woodchuck holes to check out. In addition we had woodpiles lining the field behind our home made from the bark of logs processed at the sawmill. These piles were anywhere from four to eight feet high and provided unlimited hours of adventures as we crawled through them. It was almost like an unlimited playground of ever changing topography, hidey holes, animals and whatever imaginative thing we could make from it. I think "splinters" was my middle name as a child, but that never seemed to get in the way of exploring this wonderland.

The stream nearby provided wading opportunities, tadpoles, and mud pies. When there were cattle in the fields even the electric fence became a game for the more daring.

Below our home was an old abandoned barn and blacksmith's shed. The haylofts went on forever and gave us places to explore and invent new games. The blacksmith's shop still had many of his tools and old leather, giving us new toys and adventures for many years.

Weekends were filled with family activities ranging from religious events to traditional weddings, graduations, and birthdays. If no event was planned, we were off to picnics at nearby Finger Lakes in the summer, and to each other's homes for meals and games in the winter. My immediate family living in the area numbered over 150 aunts, uncles and first cousins. And no, I do not have an accurate count, now that we are in the second and third cousin stage. Let's just say huge and I could probably stay with a relative in any of the fifty states and a few overseas countries at this time. There were large gardens at each household and pulling together for anything meant food, softball games and pinochle, the game of choice for all my aunts and uncles. We were loud, noisy, rambunctious and adventuresome.

In the winter months we were inside and pinochle was still king for the adults, but the kids were into hide/and/seek, board games, made up games, dolls, army men and whatever else our imaginations could conjure. I remember my sister and I had a very long-running airline on the stairs to the attic, where "Jean" and "Marie" the flight attendants would take care of passengers for hours. (Interesting game, given the fact that neither of us had yet been on a plane).

As young girls we did not have many dolls, but we had paper dolls, that we dressed in our own creations. Plain paper was transformed into evening gowns with crayons and scissors. Books and magazines were sources of endless information and ideas for the next project. Whether we were gluing, making papier-mache, or playing dress-up with Mom's stuff, it was a time of endless exploring and creating.

Since the area we lived in had a lot of snow, we could be gone for hours sledding the hills next to my home. I can remember coming home from a hard day of sledding and looking a little bit like a frosty cone, snow from head to foot, in our hair, cheeks red and eyes glistening from the fun we had.

When I was still fairly young, my uncle and Dad carved out a baseball field from the field next to our home. This became the gathering spot for the local kids and we all played there, regardless of age and skill level, for years on end. I can remember bringing my new husband home to his first "family" picnic after we were married where he was immediately drafted for the family game. The age range of the players was five to sixty-two, but we made it work.

We also became the beneficiaries of my uncle's vision for a swimming and fishing pond when I was around ten years old. This was every kid's dream, with a rope swing over the pond, a dock, diving board and frogs galore to chase. Late in the evenings after swimming and frogging we would build bonfires and roast marshmallows and tell ghost stories. Eventually my uncle dragged up the old blacksmith's shed and we had a cabin for slumber parties.

Our play was so much a part of our lives that it never occurred to us to get together and not play. I'll never forget my high school boyfriend's consternation when he came to my house after our graduation and there were grown men and women in high heels and suits playing hide/and/seek in the yard, in the dark. I think that was when he knew this wasn't going to be a long-term relationship, because he thought we were all crazy.

My high school years were flavored with play that expanded to cheer-leading, music, sports, and any and every other school activity I could find. The play energy from my youth spilled over to adventures that could be explored through school. Our small country high school offered a myriad of opportunities to do everything, from playing in the school band to attending science lectures at Cornell University, only twenty miles down the road. For a small country school we had teachers with strong drives to expose us to everything possible. I remember attending my first musical at Ithaca College and an opera when I was fourteen. We learned creative dance and were taken to Washington, D.C. to explore everything from the Smithsonian to Gettysburg. It was a time of learning and playing simultaneously. (Yes, Mr. Whitney we are still sorry for that particularly potent batch of sulfur dioxide we made in chemistry class, but it was fun. For those of you unfamiliar with this substance, just think rotten eggs.)

All of this did not prepare me for what was to come next.

As I left for college my mother became seriously ill, and there were some tensions in the family. While we all struggled with this new and difficult situation, we stopped playing. Life became very serious and things at home were not the same for quite some time. The play and laughter were missing for a while. More changes were looming on the horizon for me.

At college I was overwhelmed by the size of the student population, although I was attending one of the smaller colleges available to me. Getting involved in activities was much more competitive. Activities for women were almost nonexistent, since this was a men's college beginning to integrate for the first time that year. When I chose this particular school, it was, for the academic program in business that I wished to pursue. What I failed to understand and realize at the time was the need for my college to meet my need for play.

I joined the school chorus, which was coed and available. For my freshman year I also tutored in one of the poorer sections of the city with a group from the college. This ended when racial tensions flared and our site became unsafe for all involved.

My idyllic play life was slowly crawling to a halt, but I don't think I ever realized it. The "fun" became centered on parties, and those parties were centered on alcohol. It was a time of kegs and loud music. Since this was not initially my thing, (I had only had one drink up to that point in my life), I was often in the dorms with the other non-partying crew. If you remember the "geeks," well that was me. We were still playing, filling rooms with shaving cream, stringing thread and removing light bulbs to create scary spider webs for those coming in later, putting Vasoline on the toilet seats, gluing down toothbrushes, dropping water balloons; you name it, we did it. Yes, I did spend some time "grounded" by our house-mothers. It was all harmless fun, but showed that a group of us still needed to play and were having some trouble channeling it in our cloistered environment. I mean that literally, as we were housed in an old convent, with a "head nun" and local women as our housemothers who made us sign in and out every time we left the building.

Over time even the "geeks" got integrated into the party circuit, and there were less high jinks and more parties. The school provided dances and concerts, theater and other activities over time, but it was a slow process for the women. One of the gymnasiums, as an example, was the top floor of the men's dorm that was off-limits to the women. There were no intercollegiate women's activities in sports, although those came eventually. Somewhere along the line I decided to play by "working," and became one of the founding members of the "Society for the Advancement of Management" affectionately known as "SAM." This was really my only activity, which was in sharp contrast to the myriad of activities and play that I had had in my life up to this point.

Now life can intrude and take away our play in the strangest of ways, and that is what happened to me next.

The summer after my freshman year, my mother was better and I worked as a waitress for my summer job. During the day I learned to water-ski, and did so as often as possible before I had to work in the evening. It was still a fun and playful time.

In my sophomore year an arsonist burned my father and uncle's business to the ground. This was a devastating time for our family. As we rallied around each other, it became obvious that finances would be a problem while they attempted to rebuild. The summer following my sophomore year I took two jobs to make money for college that Fall.

Returning to school I immediately took a job with the University and another in the community to pay for school, room and board. I was determined to make it despite the financial setbacks. Mom and Dad in the meantime were supporting me as much as possible, but I also took out loans to make ends meet. This process continued right up to graduation and required that I get to work fast when graduation came.

At that point I was trying to support myself and pay off my loans. Play was something that I was trying to squeeze in when life was not intruding. My roommates and I were a playful bunch and would explore Boston, go to parties, and even had a weekend home on Cape Cod for one summer. It was at this point in my life that I discovered the play of the ocean. I would head to the beach every weekend, even before we had our weekend retreat, and walk the sandy beaches or body surf for the entire day. I was once again playing and doing the things that made my heart sing. After living in this area for some time, I discovered concerts on the esplanade, sporting events at the Boston Garden, fabulous ethnic restaurants, the Saturday farmer's markets, and wonderful drives along the New England coast, capped with explorations of many seacoast towns. Play was back, temporarily.

When I got married things were different. For one thing, my husband's play was very different from mine. He was a "collector" and spent many hours indoors listening to music and reading. I, on the other hand, was still full of energy, wanting to be outside and doing things at the beach, or exploring. For a while it looked like a match that may not have been made in heaven. But since love triumphs over all, we eventually found our stride in things we liked to do together, as well as apart. This was an important discovery that has lasted me all my life. To this day I still do some of my zanier playing with friends rather than my husband. This may seem strange to some, but since we have many things we enjoy doing together, doing some things apart is not a big deal.

In my twenties we were busy with starting new careers, meeting new friends and eventually moving to a new part of the country. We were into getting together with friends for sports events, and I even began doing some craftwork, which was fairly out of character for me, but fun at the time.

As my thirties dawned many things happened simultaneously. I became a rabid racquetball player, learned to ski and had two children. My career also began to take off and I was promoted continuously for many years. The children's events and activities began to be a major part of my life. I was either on the sidelines or working at sporting events, the scouts, fundraisers or musicals. Shuttling also became a big part of our lives, as the children went to parties and "play dates" with their friends. Busy became busier, then more busier.

At this time I was also of the mind that I needed to be doing my part for the world. I volunteered at a sandwich line for a food bank, became president of the Parent Teacher Association at school, became president of the local chapter of my professional association, organized a national association for one of my work vendors, helped raise money for my son's school, helped rebuild the Colorado Trail, and on and on.

The racquetball went by the wayside, the skiing became less frequent and just getting the groceries purchased and the laundry done was a major event on the weekends. Another phenomenon occurred at this time. It was escaping. For me this was having friends over for drinks and marathon games of trivial pursuit. We all waited to play on big holidays when there would be large parties and games, but the major holidays were only seven or eight times a year. While they were fun and we had many days of enjoyment, I found myself increasingly unsatisfied with how I was playing. It wasn't really my "Heart Play." Eventually even these parties went by the wayside, and we found ourselves so tired from everything that vegetating in front of a movie was the highlight of our "down" time. My "social" time became long evening phone conversations with friends while we all moaned about our work, our kids, the weather and life.

Finally it all came crashing down. My failure to stop and take time to put real "play" in my life, not occasional fun times, but real "Heart Play," led me to a painful conclusion. At first I did not even know what was happening other than a sadness that was so overwhelming that many would have called it depression. In my heart I knew that it was not depression, but an inability to live my life with the joy that I had always had before. The joy that came from play.

So out on my journey I went. The first thing that had to happen was to regain my health. In my last executive position I had worked so hard that I lost the use of my left arm from a minor injury that went untreated. Major surgery and four months of physical therapy were required to just be able to dress myself again. During this time I started to look at what I wanted on my play list. I realized that my recovery would last well into the next two years so racquetball and skiing were not really good candidates. Next, I created lists of things I thought would be fun. Half of them weren't really my ideas for fun, but things I saw others doing and enjoying and thought I should be able to enjoy, too. Slowly this list disintegrated to nothing, and I realized there was really nothing on there that I would call "Heart Play" for me.

Watching my play situation go from bad to worse was probably one of the most critical phases of getting my "Heart Play" back. By beginning to see how I was influenced by the things that others did, the more I came to realize that I was very unique as everyone is, in what I would consider play for me. Armed with this new knowledge, I decided to go back and look very carefully at my childhood play. I had to see if the secret to my play might be hidden there.

During this time I also had the opportunity to take one of those career interest tests that are so popular. I scored off the charts with the need to be outdoors. I began to think about this in light of the career I had been in for twenty some years, which required that I be indoors all the time, plus many hours of overtime. The first decision I made was to no longer work in that career, but to find a new one that would allow me to be outside more. Even if the job were indoors, it would not fill my days, and would not exclude the possibility of outdoor time.

Next, I looked at the things that made my heart sing, not only as a child, but also as an adult. This was a wonderful trip down memory lane. Slowly I was able to conjure up a picture of the things that really gave rapture and ecstasy to my life. One of them was singing. In high school and college this had been one of the most blissful activities I could imagine. Now finding where to do this became a challenge. For six months I searched and until one day the daily paper carried a special article called "Singers Wanted." In this article they described various groups around town that were looking for amateurs like myself. I joined one and started having the time of my life. The goose bumps were back!

Then I looked at my need to be outdoors. I called a landscaper to have a part of my yard ripped out and planted a garden. A garden that let me dig in the dirt with my bare hands, sort of like when I made mud pies as a kid. As you can imagine a lot of things in my life had to change for this, like loosing my lovely acrylic nails. I have never regretted that for a moment.

My dogs and I have now discovered new trails in our neighborhood to walk and enjoy the outdoors. I am going back to working on the Colorado Trail with a good friend, where we will not only enjoy the outdoors, but also laugh ourselves silly.

I finally bought furniture for a small deck off my bedroom where I can read outdoors. My work is now consulting, so on certain days I can choose to be outdoors and not indoors.

Most startling of all my discoveries was my "silence" play. I think I am fairly typical in that I watch TV and read the papers like millions of others. This is done somewhat to get information, but more so to "fill" down time. Mostly I do not like what I see on TV or read in the papers. If I really thought about it, I would have realized that I was letting someone else put thoughts into my head, even if I did not want them. What I never realized was the joy that could come from sitting in silence, without other people's ideas superimposed over my own. Letting all the noise, the work, the worry, and the "shoulds" go over for a period of time and just sitting quietly and feeling good. This has become one of my passions. I have created indoor and outdoor space to do it. I have added quiet music sometimes. I have occasionally added reading that expands my thinking, versus the simple novel. My cat joins me often and sleeps in my lap, offering her own peace to mine. During this time I often let my mind wander, to create new things to do, or even dream of new things to try. I come out of these times refreshed and joyful. I know who I am, what I like and my heart is singing.

Later you will read where I have been sledding recently, or when I saw whales in Hawaii. My play journey has been a long and sometimes painful climb, but always with a joyful outcome. Come with me while we look at how others have played, stopped playing, started again, and the miracles that are happening in their new playful lives.

2
What is Play?
Does Sleeping Count?

It is extraordinary how many different definitions of play you can find when you are asking this question. What do you think of when I say play? Swinging on a swing? Playing golf? Playing any sport you love? Cooking, visiting with friends, antiquing? Maybe none of these things, but something very special to you. No matter what you think play is there is an element common to everyone when they think of it—total and complete joy and happiness.

Play according to Webster's Dictionary is "to move lightly, rapidly, etc. (sunlight plays on the water); to engage in recreation, to take part in a game or sport; to trifle (with a thing or person); to perform on a musical instrument; to act in a drama." Recreation is further defined as "any play, amusement, etc., used to relax or refresh the body and the mind." Now there is the crux of what we are here to discover. Do we know how to relax and refresh our bodies and minds? Can we do it to such a degree that we are constantly, or almost irritatingly to our friends and business associates, filled with joy and happiness? It is possible to do so if we are really playing from our hearts.

Play is a word we use every day to describe a myriad of things. We play ball. We play games. The light plays on the crystal. We watch plays. But, what is Real Play?

It isn't as simple as Webster puts it in another dictionary definition, "to amuse or entertain oneself, to pretend to do nothing." It goes far beyond this simple definition into what we really feel when we play, what is there, and what isn't there at the moment. Sometimes what isn't there is as much of the definition as what is. This is because people look to play as a relief from the every day, from the ordinary, from the mundane. What we don't want in our play is more work, responsibility or worries. What we want is something that will make our hearts sing, souls dance and can be remembered again and again with joy and happiness.

There is a great cartoon called " One Big Happy," by Rick Detorie, where the little girl Ruthie is being picked up from a birthday party by her Dad. As she gets into the car she exclaims, "Dad you should have seen it. They had these big plastic things in the gutters so there were NO GUTTERBALLS!!! Sometimes life is so wonderful you could just mess up your hair and quack like a duck!" Now there is an example of true joy and happiness. As adults, do we have something that is so wonderful it makes us want to mess up our hair and quack like a duck?

Your own definition of play will have many elements to it, but let's start with what it was initially. As children we played **all the time.** It was a major component of our life. We played while we waited for the school bus or as we walked to school or in the car. We played during recess, and sometimes even our learning experiences were couched in play. When school was out we got into our play as fast as we could. Sports, riding our bikes, swinging, singing, video games, dolls, hide-and-seek, swimming, games, and on and on and on. We were very focused on our play because it was the purpose of our life. Healthy children are given the opportunity to play as often as possible. Toys, games, visits from friends and family were all about play. The definition to us was simple, that it wasn't homework or chores. Is our definition today that simple?

My sister Emily would say that might be close, as her definition is "no work, no responsibility." But, she goes on to say that it also needs the element of being "absolutely in the moment." This additional definition eliminates a lot of what people might consider play today, play that is more aptly defined as "escaping." Let's take a look at an all-American pastime, television. Rarely is it truly play. At best is can be minimally entertaining, but with commercial breaks and laugh tracks, I think it may be difficult to allow us to be "absolutely in the moment." (Now my husband watching a hockey game could be the exception. He is so in the moment that neither fire nor flood would "break the moment." However, given the frequent, loud invectives that send the dogs running from the room I am not sure how much fun he is really having.)

Let's go back to our childhood when play was the focus of our lives. We awoke each day and looked at our play needs and worked our "obligations" or "shoulds" around what we needed to do. Why is a child's room always messy? Because they have to play and cleaning is work. Why do children need to be reminded to take a bath? Because it interferes with playtime. Sometimes you played so hard as a child you were too tired to take a bath. Remember playing so hard that you were too tired to take a bath? What was that like? I'll bet you remember working too hard to have time for a bath!

Okay, so now we have the question, how do I know what play really means to me? In other words, what is play to me? If I go golfing I am usually having fun, but is this truly play for me? Does my heart sing, my soul dance, and am I absolutely feeling satisfied, absorbed and free? If golf were truly your "Heart Play", the answer would be yes to all these questions. But if you struggle with the sport and do it more to be with friends or as part of work, it my not be your "Heart Play".

Remember to ask, "does my heart sing, my soul dance and will I be reliving this moment in the future as play for me?" These are the many questions that define what play really is.

We are a society of leisure pursuits. Our workweek is structured so that we can work a set number of hours on a set number of days, and then have time for our "chores" followed by our time for play. Sounds like a plan, so why doesn't it work? Well, in simple terms, over a period of time women have begun to have a schedule that looks more like this: work, more work, work some more, do community service, work, help family and friends, work, work some more, sleep, eat, get dressed, get other people dressed, feed the dog and cat and bird and hamster, work, do housework, pay bills, run errands, eat in the car, deliver people to places and things to people, work, buy food, clean the house, clean the car, clean the kids, clean the neighborhood, save the rain forests, and end the day with solving world peace.

Do I exaggerate? More likely than not there are elements of every woman's life in that description. What is important as you think about play and what you want out of your life from play is to truly understand what it means to you. In other words your own definition of play, not Webster's, not my sister's (unless it fits), but your own personal journey to discover WHAT IS MY DEFINITION OF PLAY? In addition to this you must understand your life and where you spend your time, what is valuable to you in your day, and where play will fit into all of it. We will look at time for play later in this book, but right now we must find your definition of play. To do this we will look at the words and wisdom of many others who are also exploring this question.

D.C. Wincott said that "play is a creative state of withdrawal from everyday life." There are two ideas in this definition that will appear again and again throughout this book. I agree there have been, and hopefully will be, many great play moments in my life that have been very far removed from the ordinary routine of everyday life. My leap off a twenty-four foot cliff into the Colorado River is one of those moments. Despite my fear and tension at that moment, many years later I can still feel the exhilaration of floating through the air before I landed in the water. This moment of pure rapture and ecstasy that is relived on demand is something we will talk about when you begin to work on your "Heart Play."

On the other hand, I believe that play is everywhere and does not require a withdrawal from every day life, but can be built into what is required of us. We have heard people say again and again, "my work is my play." I said it myself for years, and it was true, up to a point. My work right now, writing this book, is very often more fun and play than work.

In my previous career there were many things that were very playful for me in my work also. When we look at the "Blessing of Playful Life" at the end of this book, you will see where women who have wholly integrated play into their lives are definitely playing at work, as well as outside of work.

Another way of looking at work as play is sometimes just the approach we take to our workplace, even though the work may be far from playful. One of my clients has a secretary that wears the wildest slippers you have ever seen while sitting at her desk. Her head is working; her feet are stuck in playfulness. The woman is always smiling. I think I know why. Another person I know has a desk full of wind-up walkers that she uses for comic relief when the work is not play, and she needs to play now. Walking into her office when they are all going at the same time is quite the play experience.

Work for some people can be an intensely creative experience. Intense creativity is actually one form of play. As an example, you may have had the opportunity to make or create a Halloween costume for yourself or a child. This can be an intensely creative process bringing you joy and happiness. I think we should be required to create a costume once a year, even if it is as simple as wearing your shirt or dress backwards. It requires us to engage that creative side of us that may have been dormant too long. It would also create an opportunity for us to look at what is playful to us. Would we dress up as tennis pros? Maybe a queen or a king? How about an ant? (Crawling on the ground is what we thought was play as a child). Would we paint, sew, build, or paste in the process of creating this costume? As we did those things, what would it tell us about our definition of play? When we are creating at work, something as simple as a new spreadsheet or solving a problem, if we are being intensely creative, we may be playing too.

If we define our play based on our life experiences and what we want in our lives in the future, we begin to understand one of the key elements needed to get more play into our lives. Play is something that gives life a sharper focus. Rather than going through each day with the "shoulds", play gives you a break and focuses you on who you really are. Ovid once said " in our play we reveal what kind of person we really are." So the question is, what kind of person are you? Can we look at your play, your definition of play, and truly know you? Maybe rather than going through premarital counseling we just need each person to define their idea of play and how they practice it and we will know everything we need about our future spouse!

Now we have to stop here and talk to all those people who have read this far and are cringing inside because they think that taking time to play or having play in their lives might be selfish. This feeling is fairly dominant in the responsible, adult female.

There is a great teacher, Abraham, who speaks through Esther Hicks (Abraham-hicks.com), who has some great thoughts on selfishness. In a nutshell, she says, "bring it on!" The thought here is that the definition of selfishness is to "take care of self." Play is often considered selfish, and therefore left out of life, or minimized. Is this really the right thing to do? What if life was really about playing and the rest was the sidebar? What if when we are through on this planet the real question is "Did you have fun?" Now there is an inspiration for taking a really good look at what we think play is, when we do it and whom we do it with.

In the documentary, The Promise of Play, sponsored by the American Toy Institute and the Institute for Play in California, Jane Goodall does a sequence where she talks about adult primates interacting and "playing" with their young, and its correlation with the leadership that is later demonstrated by the young as adults. There were without a doubt, better and healthier attitudes in those young who were raised with play as a foundation of their lives. In fact the entire Institute for Play is devoted to the research and education of people about the importance of play for good mental health.

Play is something that happens in what Diane Ackerman refers to as a "special mental place." This is a critical component in understanding our definition of play. I have observed that there is great mental concentration, to the exclusion of thinking about anything else in our lives, when we play appropriately. Have you ever noticed the child that sits and builds with blocks and the focus that they will put into that event? You would think that the Taj Mahal was under construction. How about when a softball team is out there on a summer evening? The events of ordinary life are left behind for a few brief moments while they focus on the ball.

These are examples of total focus that bring joy and happiness into the lives of the people involved. You also see this focus in a good hairstylist when they create a new style. That is play at work through creating. You have seen this focus when a chef is inspired to try new ingredients in an old recipe. They focus on what they love to do and the result is joy. There is the person riding their bike, painting a picture or hugging a tree, who is playing and smiling and filling their heart with joy.

Of the many women who shared their thoughts with me about play for this book each had their own idea and definition of play. You could tell that they looked at the opportunities that are presented to them to play and applied their personal definitions before they decided whether the activity was play for them. Many of their words were the same, many were unique, and all were honest. Their comments may reflect some of your own.

"Play to me is relaxing, pursuing things that bring pleasure and I try to weave it through everything I do."

"When you are playing you are so in the moment that nothing else matters."

"When I am learning, I am playing and vice versa."

"Play for me means there is no objective to what I am doing. It is a process of being totally abandoned in what you are doing."

"When I am playing I am moving, feeling alive, laughing and smiling."

"Play for me means having fun doing nothing, the result is irrelevant."

"Play cannot involve competition and while I am playing I cannot find time to think about any concern or problem."

"Play takes you to a place where you are totally comfortable."

Now you must stop and think about what play is to you. You have heard from others. You have read several definitions from the dictionary. You may know what your kids think play is, what your spouse thinks play is, but the question is, what do you think play is? Finding your own definition of play may not be as simple as reading the words here and then formulating a thought. As I mentioned in my story earlier, this is a journey, where your definition of play may take time to find, and may grow and change as you grow and change. Much of the fun will be in the journey. Be open to seeing other people play and asking yourself the question, "would that be play for me?" We all have warehouses of the things we "thought" might be fun, but turned out only to be "amusements." So it is with our definition of play. What we think play is may only be what amuses us. We need to find our real definition of play, for our unique lives.

3
Why Do We Need To Play? We Have Enough To Do!

Quite often I will hear the following comment from someone when I begin to talk about play, "I see no good reason to play. My life is complete with good work, a wonderful family, good friends that I see often and enjoy their company, community service and small entertainments like reading and television that help me relax." What is this playing thing all about?

We need to play because there is more for us to learn and know about our selves hidden in our play. There is growth we have yet to go through, there are issues we have yet to deal with, and there are good times that are inside us dying to come out that haven't been given a chance. Quite simply, there is more for us to do with our lives than we are doing now. In those things there are solutions to the little problems and dilemmas of life. Maybe if we play hard enough and well enough there will be solutions to larger problems, like violence and hunger. Am I being too flippant? No. We are incapable of solving big or little problems if we are not fully present in the moment and sure of ourselves. There is a need, a longing, a desire to be everything we are and much, much more that can be explored with play.

If you have worked in any American business in the last five years, you most likely have been subjected to one or more programs on creative problem-solving. The premise of these are all the same, to get people to think differently about problems and come up with new and better solutions. You have seen people dangling on ropes, climbing trees, sleeping on mountaintops, dancing on table tops. Companies will bring in clowns, circus performers or whatever it takes to get the juices going. What always amazes me about these programs is that the same people who hire us to come and teach people to play and be creative refuse to allow any play in the day-to-day workplace. It doesn't work that way. You need to play all the time. It needs to be your frame of mind. How can this be more fun? What can I play to make myself feel better, thus think better and do better at life?

We need to play because life is serious. It ends up "dead" serious. And dead serious is not fun. My admired friend Alan Cohen once pronounced in one of his workshops that "we should live life with so much joy that when we die we will not notice it." It is my motto for life. I want to have joy in every minute of everything. Does it happen? No. But, can it happen? Yes, if I work hard enough at it and know what play is to me.

Even while writing this book I was stayed in a condominium in Steamboat Springs, Colorado and had planned total solitude for a week to get it done. I grocery shopped and stocked my refrigerator, not planning to go out much except to exercise and seek inspiration on the banks of the Yampa River. Lo and behold the universe had other plans in mind for me. On the second day of my stay I discovered it was warmer in the refrigerator than in the condo. Thus began a two day parade of people who poked and probed that refrigerator until it was officially declared dead. Play? Joy? Fun? You bet. The people who came through were delightful and even inspirational when it came to helping me with the book. Dave is even quoted in the book as the mysterious "mountain sage." The word got around I was working on this book and even the daily housekeeper had something to offer. Play is everywhere. We had a lot of fun.

We need to play because it makes all the difference in our health, wealth and joy. Can play really be this influential, can it really make that much difference? If I work really, really hard, can I not have wealth which will give me joy? If I eat right and exercise, won't I keep my health even if I do not play? There is the possibility that working hard and taking care of ourselves physically can give us a degree of health, wealth and joy, but what I am referring to in the real reason for play is the right to extraordinary health, extraordinary wealth and extraordinary joy. It is no longer good enough to just be healthy, we want to be strong. We want the skill and ability to do whatever will come our way. Climb mountains? No problem! Swim rivers, lakes, oceans? No problem. Stay up to see the sunrise at Machu Picchu? No problem. We as human beings have the desire to get out, to go, to do. We want to be able to run, jump and swing all the way up to the end. And good "Heart Play" is a way for us to get there.

Sure we want enough wealth to feed, clothe and shelter ourselves and our families, but we also want to take trips and buy occasional extravagances. We deserve the opportunity to fund our good ideas and see them played out. Paint a room, buy a car, travel to a foreign country, own gold or gemstones, give to good charities. All are natural and healthy wishes for the use of wealth. To get the wealth we have to play in a way that leads to these things.

There is a great deal written these days about not living with a feeling of lack, but living instead with a feeling of prosperity. This feeling of prosperity comes from creating a feeling of wealth with what we have. Appreciating what we have can be found in our play. Recently, I was at a park where many people who would not fit the Wall Street Journal definition of wealthy, had gathered for the day. There were piles of ethnic food for munching all day, a volleyball game, someone leading a sing-a-long of fun songs on the guitar, kids on patched inner tubes floating along the shallow creek, other kids finding creatures on the creek bank, a card game and so on. This was one of the wealthiest groups of people I have seen in a long time and their "play" was their banker.

What about the wealth of peace and serenity? The wealth in our hearts that we want to nurture and sometimes share? The wealth that is knowing we are doing the right thing for ourselves? The wealth of giving and receiving the love that is yours to give and receive? Not all wealth is monetary. There is great wealth in the overwhelming sense of being exactly who you want to be and allowing yourself all the luxuries that come with that allowing. It is a sense of wealth and prosperity that comes to those who have decided to lead with their heart and not their head or their checkbook. When they lead with their heart they find the play which makes their heart sing, the work which nourishes their minds and their pocketbooks, and the joy in each thing they do.

How often have you found yourself at a social or family obligation that is completely contrary to what you would like to be doing at that moment in time? How often have you made your weekly schedule and taken a conscious look at what will be totally playful and fun and scheduled that first, before work, obligations and chores?

Wealth is something that must be redefined and totally understood before you can truly commit to your "Heart Play" and feel the rewards of your wealth. You must trust and know that you are a person who is not just here to go to work five or six or seven days a week, cook and clean, and occasionally take a few moments to relax and have fun. You want your life to be full of joy. Full of life. Full of love.

Remember when you didn't do your chores? It was because you got distracted with your play. Now here is the point where your mind starts telling you that all this is fine and dandy, but Mom and Dad were off making money for food, cooking the meals, running to the store and paying the bills, so the child had time to play. True. But as adults we have taken all these tasks and obligations to the extreme to the detriment of the play inside that NEEDS TO COME OUT! Yes, here is the crux of why we really need to play.

Earlier we quoted Ovid, when he said, "In our play we reveal the kind of person we really are." Now it is time to figure out who that is, because quite simply we will not have the JOY we want in our lives if we refuse to be honest and play. Notice I said be honest in addition to play. Believe it or not, we are going to have to look at ourselves and see what we do each day HONESTLY before we can understand how and when to play. Why? Unless we are willing to look at all the activities that we do to please others or because we think they SHOULD be done, we will never hear what we honestly would like to do and when we honestly would have the time to do it. Let me give you several examples of this.

Carol is a person of strong integrity and a great sense of duty to friends and family. She is always there for everyone who needs her and gets many compliments for her efforts. She feels good about these compliments and uses them to support her continued devoted service to both. Most of the things that Carol does for these people are also things they are capable of doing without her, but it is easier to do them with her. The question to Carol is how does she honestly feel about doing all these things, which eat up the free time she has outside of work and personal obligations? She will immediately respond when asked that she feels fine. She is doing a service for people who need her, she enjoys their company and it gives her a sense of accomplishment. An almost honest answer. It is almost honest because she has been trained to think that is the best answer and to say anything else would seem SELFISH. There actually was another answer that Carol had when pressed. Although she does feel "fine" and she does enjoy her family "most of the time," she resents her loss of free, "play" time. If there is even a little niggling of resentment, we are not being honest with ourselves. We need to admit that we really do have to play more, but are stuck with time problems.

How often do we hear after the weekend, the exclamation of "Where did it go? Why am I so tired? Nothing got done!" Where is our playtime? Was the only play snoozing in front of a rented movie at the end of the day? Twenty minutes of catch with one of the kids? Attending an event that you felt obligated to attend? We have to become very honest with ourselves and look at where and how we spend our time to get to the wealth, health and joy we so richly deserve in this life.

Another example is Susan. She is busily trying to get the wealth she deserves by working very, very hard and supporting her family as a single parent. She is industrious, talented and busier than a bee in the height of it's season, fifty weeks a year. She is always one step behind and always a little bit unhappy. I have seen this person in what would and should have been the best moments of her life, not really able to feel and enjoy those moments with what little energy she had left for these glorious times. Her energy had been drained off through long work hours and obligations to others. She rarely "plays" for herself, but is well known for being available for others when they need someone to go along. Often she goes along to see if she can squeeze some play in her life, but it is their "Heart Play" not hers, so it does not have the feeling of joy, only fun. Fun is not bad, it is better than nothing, but let us be clear early on that fun is very different from joy.

Joy is the ability to feel your heart sing. The ability for you to feel so good that you absolutely cannot stop grinning. The ability to feel warm all over. When you are through playing you are able to retrieve the experience from your memory bank and relive it. You are able to recapture the moment with joy all over again. When you think about your play you can focus on it and feel instantly refreshed. Your play opens your heart. When your heart is open you open your eyes and see things for what they really are. Your spirit is opened and you can feel everything to a greater degree. You are no longer numb to the world, but experiencing it fully and with great glee.

Susan has fun in her life, all you need to do is ask her. Does she have joy? Maybe. The choice to not create the time for play, to believe that working longer and harder is the only answer to wealth, and to continue to have "fun" as a substitute for joy may keep her from ever having real wealth, extraordinary health and joy. Colds and flu may plague her as "part of life." There will always be a shortage of money, even after more comes into her life and she owns more things. And finally when she wakes up in the morning she will be driven to do what needs to be done that day and more, and in the end she will not be able to smile with joy as she closes her eyes for rest.

I have been accused of being everything from Pollyanna to just plain nuts when I discuss my belief that we have a right to play and that it can bring great things to our lives. I accept this criticism, and it drives me on to find more and more reasons and examples to prove that I am right. After all, Pollyanna went on to live a wonderful and glorious life.

Not too long ago I encountered a woman who looked at me tearfully and said, " I am just a workaholic. I never play, I don't know how to play, and I am gravely unhappy." As we explored this person's life it was obvious that she did indeed work a great deal. The woman was at the top in her company, then after a merger became subordinate to someone else. Although not a demotion in the technical sense of the word—same title, same pay, same office—a demotion it was nonetheless. She was no longer the boss. Her work ethic kicked in at that point and she has been on over-load for the last three years. She works hard, long and longer to prove her worth.

The first thing we discovered when we began to examine her life is that she had put some playful, fun things in her life, but due to working so hard she was forgetting to enjoy them. Her massages and manicures, were a lot of fun if done in the right spirit. In other words, a massage deserves your full attention, before, during and after. I even know a place in Santa Fe, New Mexico that has a sign requesting that clients get relaxed *before* coming into the massage and four or five ways to do so. (e.g. hot tub, meditation, yoga or tai chi,.). Once you have had a good massage it is important to let the benefits seep through your system. Let your muscles and your brain enjoy the pampering it has just received. Racing back to work or the next "thing" you have to do just doesn't cut it and can negate the entire experience.

The second thing we discovered was that she really did not have a clue as to what her "Heart Play" would be, even if she had the time. This reminded me of a wonderful saying that tells us that "we don't stop playing because we got old, we grow old because we stop playing." (C. Wyatt Runyan) We will get old. Our bodies will age. But, we have the option of making old as playful as young. It can also be more enjoyable because we are smarter, and have many more resources available to us than when we were kids.

As I worked with this individual she began to explore all the things from her childhood she liked to do. She looked at all the things she would have liked to have done, but was either afraid or too busy to do. Then she set about finding her "Heart Play." In the process you could almost see her "reverse aging." Sure she still has wrinkles, but now the light in her eyes reflects so brightly you barely notice them. She is someone you want to be around and someone you want to share adventures with. All I could think of as she went through this process is how fortunate she was to have taken the time to give herself the play she deserved. Her health, wealth and joy began to magnify every day.

The effects of play on our health should not be underestimated. To illustrate there is the story of Helen. When Helen was forty-four years of age she became very, very ill. Her lungs had sustained serious damage from a severe childhood bout with pneumonia. In serious distress, breathing difficulties landed her in the emergency room close to death many times. She was treated with all the modern drugs available, given an inhaler, and was forced to seriously curtail her activities, during the harsh winters where she lived. After living with this difficulty for many years she was struck with colon cancer, which she beat. Today she is a very healthy 79-year-old woman. How is this possible when doctors and observers were predicting her demise earlier? The answer is simple, Helen knows how to play. She plays a wicked game of cards. She challenges herself with the television show "Who Wants To Be A Millionaire" whenever it is on. She has a frightfully hard puzzle waiting for you if you visit her home. You will be laughing and cursing within the hour as you try to solve it. When her friends lock doors and batten hatches against the winter's blast, she is in the car with her partner and off south to walk the beaches, pick fresh fruit, shop, swim, play more cards, check out the stores or whatever strikes her fancy that day.

The woman tires me out with her play and I should know, because she is my mother. She has her health because she chooses consciously to have play in her life. Because my mother ignored the early symptoms of cancer, the colon surgery was a life and death effort. I will never forget my father standing outside her room before surgery, saying she has to survive because they had not done all the things they had yet to do together. And he was right. They have had many, many more years of playing since that time. When I was a child playing my mother could rarely contain herself from joining in. She still does it. Okay, so she can't run the bases in the family softball games anymore, but she can sit behind the backstop and give the umpire a hard time, if she wants to. Sometimes our health is so wrapped up in our play that we do not even know it. Could the cure for whatever ails us be in our "Heart Play?" We won't know until we try it.

Where is the joy in our lives? Play unlocks that mystical, magical place so wonderful that we want to stay there forever. Joy is one of the main reasons that we play.

I recently noticed a group of people staring at a young child. This child had the biggest smile you had ever seen. He was deliriously happy about some small wonderment in life and was expressing his joy through his smile. We do that too as adults, just not as often. We want this childlike joy back in our lives. If there were no other reason to play, no improved health, nor greater wealth, other than joy, I would still be the first in line to get some.

It is so obvious to me, when I meet people and talk to them about play, who is really playing and who is not. I meet many "happy" people who are not playing very much. They are content, friendly and smiling. When I meet people who have found and live their "Heart Play" they not only smile, they beam! You can see and feel the joy they have in their lives. After a few minutes of conversation with them they will very excitedly share their joy with you as they describe their "Heart Play." You've seen this before in kids with an animated narration of the frog they caught, the game they won or the new dance step they learned.. This is the true joy of "Heart Play."

One person I met this past year, Ruth, made my heart sing just to be in the room with her. She has made her "Heart Play" her work and she radiates joy through every pore. Her eyes sparkle and her smile lights up a room. After people have met Ruth they never forget her or the joy she has in her life. Ruth works in a profession that allows her to give of herself through healing. She also leads people on explorations for spiritual growth and is constantly taking herself on explorations for more spiritual growth.

While not all of us may be able to make our play our work, we can give ourselves permission to play more and bring that light into our own eyes.

There is another good reason to play. Life can be tough. It throws curve balls when we least expect it. We can be saddled with trying to get back our old feelings of well being after a difficult time. A woman I know was struggling with just such a time in her life when she created what she called "the ultimate play experience," for herself and her friends. On New Year's Eve she rented an apartment on the Mall in Denver, Colorado where the 2001 New Year was going to be celebrated with one of the largest fireworks displays in the country. The energy of the crowd on the mall, accompanied by a visual show that delighted the most jaded of observers, made the evening memorable for everyone who attended. It was truly "Heart Play" that helped to refocus and re-energize her past the difficult experience.

How had we as children turned to play to heal the wounds of traumas, big or small? Children know instinctively to get on with their lives after a difficult time. They know that play will take them somewhere safe to heal and refocus before they may go on in a healthy way. Do we as adults know enough to do this, or do we think it almost criminal to play when something terrible has just happened? Play and healing life's wounds go hand in hand.

One last good reason to play, and one of my favorites, is that playing will help us find the work that we love. Have you ever looked at someone with a really spectacular job and wished it were you? Well, it can be.

When we truly give our attention to our "Heart Play" we will begin to see the skills and talents we have in that area. With the right thinking and belief in ourselves, there may be new career opportunities waiting for us as defined by our play. This isn't as far fetched as it seems. Everyone knows at least one person who has taken their play into a job. Someone who loves music could be working for a record company or playing in an orchestra. Someone who loves flowers and gardening may be running their own shop. Someone who loves people and being outside of an office sells Real Estate. Someone who loves books is working in a library or bookstore. Someone who likes to build things is running their own building company. Golf pros, piano tuners, hairstylists, and on and on. If you have any doubts about looking more into your "Heart Play", do it for no other reason than to find the work you love.

4

Our Childhood Play, When It Came So Easy

Understanding how we played as children and what we liked and didn't like are a big part of bringing back play into our adult lives. Childhood play contains all the elements of who we were and what we liked to do. It tells about the things that came naturally to us. It also tells us what we did with the things that were at our disposal. Some of us were raised in cities, with streets full of friends and adventure. Others came from small towns, and some from the country. Some children lived in many different environments as their parents moved from place to place.

Let me give you an example. I grew up in the country, but not on a farm. The hamlet of Catatonk was a whistle stop for the train and had around twenty houses scattered beside a highway connecting Ithaca with New York City, three hours away. We had acres and acres of land and forest around us, but that was pretty much it. One thing we had for the first few years of my life was my father's sawmill in this same area. They cut the bark off trees (slab wood) and hauled it to a field behind our house where it was unloaded to await further use or be burned. These slab piles went on forever, and created a magical kingdom for myself and my cousins who lived just down from our house. We would go into these piles heedless of the snakes and bugs and rodents who also claimed them as home, and made forts, built hideaways, created mysterious places and filled them with all manners of utensils we had fashioned out of the wood. Our parents would spend hours calling us for chores while we hid away in our domain. We used what we had to create a fabulous world for ourselves. To this day, I have never had a toy as a child or adult that was as much fun as that old wood. It is a warm and precious memory for me. It is also a memory that tells me what I like to do. I like to be outdoors, I like to create and I like to be with good friends on adventures.

So many of the women I interviewed have told me stories about the gang getting together to ride bikes and climb trees. These women were almost always in motion. Women's play stories seem to contain a common element of "always into something," pretending, exploring and creating.

One woman related her childhood play to me as "whatever happened when you went out the front door." She meant that she reacted to the day with spontaneity and adventure. I liked her story about always playing detectives and trying to get the bad guys. The bad guys were always "larger than life," what kids are looking for in their play. She said every game had some element of this "larger-than-life problem to it." Even when they played store, they got robbed and had to check the clues and find the criminal. When a real mobster's funeral was held in her neighborhood, she and her friends were so excited the funeral procession could barely get through all the bicycles from the curious kids!

Curiosity, larger-than-life, explorations are the basics of much of our childhood play. In my interviews with women, I heard the story of "hitting the front door and letting it happen" over and over again. Play was a very "in the moment" type of thing that depended on the weather, who was available that day, and what caught their attention. These beginnings in play tell us a lot about who we are going to be as playful adults. They can tell us about what we were like when people weren't telling us where to go, do or be somewhere or something all the time. You know, the time before you had a job, a family, community commitments, animals to care for, plants to water and so on.

One of the most productive things about going back and reliving our childhood play is recapturing the way we felt when we were playing. It is sometimes difficult to figure out our adult "Heart Play" because we have forgotten the joy that was created with complete abandonment as a child. By going back and reliving the moments of our childhood that were pure joy, we can then find our adult play activities that enable a similar feeling.

I met a woman in her late twenties who played with her Barbie dolls as a child. These were her favorite things in the world, and she still has her whole collection to this day. She was recently married and trying to figure out how and when to bring them back out without scaring her new husband. Sometimes childhood comes right along with us into adulthood and that is not necessarily bad. She is a very successful business professional and levelheaded in most things. She is also struggling to get play back into her life. We will visit her story again a little later in this book, but know for now that looking at and remembering her fun with dolls is helping her search for play as an adult.

Many women are surprised when they look at their childhood play and see how much they left behind. Riding bikes is always high on the list. Singing with girlfriends to songs on the radio, dancing like crazy when good rollicking music comes on. These are things we never wanted to stop doing, but did. The sheer physicality of play is something that is very different for most women in childhood and adult play. Girls are usually head-to- head with the boys in the swimming, swinging, biking, climbing and running categories. This changes over time to more sedentary play for the girls, while the boys are still fairly physical. This is neither a good nor a bad thing, as we will discuss later in looking at gender differences in play. It does however create some confusion for women as they grow up and look for those same joyful childhood experiences to find that women's play is not as active as their male counterparts.

The more we reminisce about our play, the more different places and things come into our minds. Some people had a sandbox or swing set to play on, while others had special identities. Board games and games like Gossip and silly made-up games come to mind. Our imaginations were a big part of our play as children; it was used constantly to enliven the day, our games and life in general. I can remember catching tadpoles and lightning bugs until our laundry room looked like a science lab. The jars would line the counter and floor while my mother pleaded for the freedom of the creatures. This usually spurred us on to add crickets and daddy long legs to make the collection complete. My mother had many canning jar lids with holes in them by the end of the summer. What was it about capturing a lightning bug that was so exciting that we would stay outside, for hours, being eaten alive by mosquitoes, while we waited for another one to come by our jar? What is it now that will cause us to go through waiting and bug bites or some other inconvenience for the joy it brings?

I had to laugh at myself after a recent camping trip with a good friend. Over the years it seems that we do become less tolerant of life's discomforts, (e.g. mosquitoes, sleeping on the hard ground, being cold). Our gear for this two-night trip filled not only the cargo space in the back of her SUV but the back seat as well, and we weren't even bringing the food! Foam pads, extra clothing, solar shower, we were going to be comfortable no matter how much gear it took. Despite all this the ground was still hard, the night freezing cold, and the bugs found their way into everything. Did we play? You bet. It was worth every bit of discomfort to be with good friends, hike in the beautiful mountains and sleep under the stars next to a rushing river. While what I will endure for play has changed, my ability and desire to still have these play moments gives me the stamina to put up with the discomforts of the territory.

My childhood added even more fuel to our play fires, as we were surrounded by hills, hills and more hills and could sled forever, which we did. Despite the shortened days we did snow forts, sledding and snowball fights until dusk settled and we had to go inside. We were frozen to the core and tired, but happy beyond belief. What would you do now that would make you put up with the cold and the wet to find joy?

Many people struggle with play as adults because of the reactions or feedback given to them as children. I recently ran into someone from my childhood who had a terrible reputation from birth as being a "troublemaker."

Now, I must admit as a child I always liked this kid because he was experimenting, trying new things. This opinion comes even after I awarded him my "most difficult person to baby sit award." Sometimes things got a little out of hand, but it was never tragic. He would get the dog wet, be particularly loud, maybe trample a bush or get very dirty. The problem was that he always received feedback from his mother and father that it was BIG stuff. In his adult years he is not very playful. He has a good life, but as I spoke to him I could not help but notice the lack of a gleam or twinkle in his eye. I wonder how much his life now is shaped by the judgments about his play and energy as a child?

We are so quick to label children as troublemakers, spoiled, "bad kids" and much more. What is the message that you received about your play as a child? Did your parents encourage play? Discourage play? Did they criticize the mess you made rather than see the creation coming out of the mess? We may need to give ourselves permission to play again; free from criticism, so we know what play feels like in a positive way. A good way to start is to buy some finger paints and paper and just have at it. I tried using this method with someone who had negative feedback about play as a child. They very carefully put one finger in the paint jars and drew pictures in straight lines all over the page. I asked if they ever thought of taking a big glob of the paint and smearing it, then creating a picture in the smear. They looked at me in total consternation, saying that it never occurred to them to play that freely with the paints. Give yourself the finger paint test to see what you need to do to be free to play.

We see a recurrent theme of how others react to our play, and subsequently what we choose to do for play, in the teens and young adult life. Peer pressure from teenage friends has curbed many playful moments. I have even seen parents still attempting to curb play through loud disapproval when their children are in their twenties and thirties.

Our childhood play also encompasses the difficulties of life. One woman explained that in her home her alcoholic father had a definite influence on the amount of play and the level of engagement. If he was not present the kids were rambunctious and noisy and generally played gleefully. When he was around he demanded quiet and decorum, so the children made games that could be played under the blankets or bed. It is amazing the resiliency that children show for their play in the face of difficulty. The question we have for ourselves as adults is do we have that same resiliency for play in the midst of the difficulties that life will inevitably throw at us?

Children are worth observing as we go through this journey of life and attempt to hold onto play as adults. They honor their play as the sole and only purpose of each day when they get up. They have the tools for it, either from the local toy store or the cabinet in the kitchen. They have the time for it. They have the energy for it and know that it is the right thing to do with their time.

It is important that we look at our childhood play for what it is. It is the past, and does not necessarily determine what our future will be. It tells us what we were like, the good and sometimes the bad. It gives us clues about what we might want to be doing now, and what we left behind as we grew up to be adults. Let yourself enjoy this walk down memory lane and make notes when you get that good feeling about something you did as a child. Later, you can reflect on how you can recreate those feelings today in your play.

When you are writing a book on play, you do not necessarily want to talk about some of the more painful aspects of life. But there are always exceptions and reasons for those exceptions. In interviewing many women our discussions of childhood play brought up some very painful memories, abuse, alcoholism, a parent's serious illness, angry parents, parents struggling to survive, parents who were remote and uninvolved and many other difficult stories. By going back and looking at childhood play, we sometimes resurrect the difficult feelings that went with them. Hiding in the closet to play, not being able to make noise, not being allowed to get messy, the lack of play, hiding in a log or the car or under the bed, many of these things fit our childhood play profile. Rather than dredge up old bad memories however, these times and situations show us resilience. We are able to take the tougher things and turn them into better things for ourselves in our current life. Alan Cohen's infamous saying is that "your history is not your destiny." In this simple phrase we learn that the traumas of childhood do not have to plague us as adults. We can learn to go on despite what happened yesterday. For those of you who recognize some of this trauma when looking back at your childhood, take care to find the play and the strength that you had and make a better playful time for yourself, now as an adult. Remember, what has happened in the past is not what will happen in the future. Go play and have some fun.

5

Messages That Didn't Come in a Bottle

Becoming Women—The Teen Years

As we left our childhood play and became young women, we discovered many hidden messages that came to us. Where they came from is somewhat unknown. When my sister tried to figure out why she stopped playing baseball in the field behind our home, she could not point to a singular cause. It just happened. Was it because the boys were now all on school teams? Was it because she would look like a tomboy if she continued to play sandlot baseball? Was she busy with new pursuits? Where did she receive the message to stop playing something she loved?

An interesting change in play occurs when little girls become adolescents and then teenagers. Too often play begins to disappear. In my seminars with women we always ask when play seemed to stop or slowdown or disappear? Inevitably we find that between the ages 11 to 14 young girls begin to play less.

A colleague of mine told me that she loved to draw and paint as a child and so good at it had won the top award for art in her state when she was in the sixth grade. She never painted or drew again. When I asked her why, she explained that the art classes in junior high and high school were considered "uncool" by her friends and thus she did not enroll. Are girls more susceptible to the thoughts and perceptions of others and thus leave behind their likes and "play" quicker than boys or are boys just as likely to do the same thing? We will discuss this more in the chapter on gender differences in adult play.

In the inventory I did with many women, I found the teen years to be bleak at best when it came to play. One woman told me she could not remember one thing that she had done for play as a teenager and had given up everything from her childhood. She seemed both startled and dismayed that her teen years would not have had play in them. Her question to herself was " What was I doing?" My question is what did this do to her "play-ability?" Did she lose the ability to play during that time, making her path to play now so much harder? Is the ability to play something that can be lost if not practiced, like muscle tone from the lack of exercise?

It is important to look at the messages that little girls receive as they become young women and adults. The message about play seems to be that as we age we need to get more responsible and stop playing. Ever heard that one? I heard it very cryptically when I was told that Saturday mornings could no longer be spent playing at my father's factory, but that I instead must stay home and do housework with my mother. This included cleaning, baking and polishing in preparation for Sunday, a day of rest. My mother was not being mean-spirited and was not wrong in her expectation for me. This is how she had been raised—she believed it was right and she was only being a good mother. The fact that my little-girl heart was broken affected my attitude for a long time after that. My "play-ability" was being compromised, but I didn't really understand what to do about it.

As a growing young woman I was never fully comfortable in traditional roles that excluded play. For that reason I was seen as rebellious, inconsiderate and even rude. My mother will tell you, I was not a fun teenager for her to raise. I wanted to play all the time. I missed my slab pile, my softball games, sledding and riding the carts in my father's factory. I probably would have continued to do all those things if I had not been reined in. Now there is a scary thought. I realize that many people think that giggly teenage girls are a major annoyance, but look at what they are trying to bring into their lives, play—a sense of fun and freedom that they had as little girls, but now are struggling to find in their adolescence.

Diane told me that as a little girl and a young woman she had a disproportionate share of the household chores relative to her brother. He had the "occasional" chore and yet she was expected to help with everything from cooking to cleaning and beyond. As she hit her teen years her mother returned to the workforce and Diane added preparing dinner and caring for the family to her list. Her brother was not expected to contribute in the same way. Diane is not resentful of any of this; she states it as a fact. She was and is now capable of bringing fun and play into her life. Nonetheless, the rules were different for her and her brother.

April relates a similar story in her teen years. Her father became disabled and her mother had to return to the workforce. In her case her older sister was already in college and her brother was only nine, so she became responsible for running the house. Remarkably April never resented this intrusion to her extremely active play life. She was required to give up tennis lessons, swimming and many other outside activities to run the house. She found these times called upon her to create a new way to play, in the house, and with what was available to her. To that end April has a highly developed sense of play that she uses with her daughters today. If you walk by their home on the weekends you will see two adults and two little girls dancing and singing and whirling around the living room, having the time of their lives.

Beth was a Barbie child. She lived for her dolls and their games. Her collection was large and her pride and joy. (Notice that word joy). Beth told me that she was approached by her mother one day to perhaps put her Barbie dolls away. Her mother did not insist, only mentioned that it might be time. The only problem with the request was that Beth was not ready to put them away. How many times as adults do we pick when a child should or should not "grow up?" We are told by the "wise" adults when it is time to put away your childish things and become an adult. I did not receive a Barbie doll when they came out because I was "too old" that year for toys for Christmas. Don't worry I own one now and she is staring at me as I write these words, offering encouragement.

My sons recently revealed to me that I could not use our sub-basement to store some things for my seminars because it was "full." "Full of what?" I replied. "Toys!" they exclaimed. When I said the typical mother thing of, "aren't you a little old for that?" they promptly informed me that these were valuable possessions they planned to preserve for their potential "antique" value at a later date. They weren't fooling me, I have seen my sons go down there and be absorbed for hours with these toys even though they are both adults. They sneak down there and play. I have always given my children toys for Christmas. Age should not matter when it comes to toys or play; the ability to play is what is important.

We, as a society, can be very sober, serious and responsible. We know what needs to be done and we do it, for the most part. Play has been a compartmentalized place for most with rules to abide by. Think how contrary that is to what we discussed in childhood play. We emphasized the spontaneity of childhood play. As the teen years approach a lot of this play becomes more regulated. Competitive sports, theater, games that have set rules, not the ones we made up that day, and structured events. Think back to the words that we used in describing childhood play and our definitions of play. We talked about hitting the front door and doing whatever lay before us. We talked about being in the moment. We talked about no work or responsibilities.

Is it possible that as we were being raised that we were weaned from play the same way we were weaned from a bottle? Before I gave an example of my parent's message to do responsible things rather than play. Brandi's mother also gave her a very direct message. Other messages people have told me of were subtler. As I mentioned previously, when women were asked to look at their play history and tell me when they stopped playing, they all came in somewhere around the ages of eleven to fourteen. This is fairly consistent with most women. When we put the dolls away, for whatever reason, what did we pick up to replace them? One person told me they could not think of one thing they played in junior high or high school. Others said they went into sports or chorus or drama, but on a touch-and-go basis. It was not a fundamental part of their day. They did not wake up thinking what will I play at today? For some women it was all about grades and studying to get into the right school. For some it was about make-up and clothes and music. For some it was about boys and boys and boys. I am an avid cartoon reader, if you have not figured that out yet, and I love the cartoon *Luann* by Greg Evans. Luann's teenage angst portrays the boredom and restlessness of the teenage years very well. But, look more closely and you will also see the total and complete lack of play in and around her. Once again, the dolls have been put away and besides boys, make-up, music and clothes, where is the play?

My sister and I were fortunate to grow up in a small high school that never had enough kids to populate all the things that were available, so we were able to be in band, chorus, cheerleaders, Girl's Athletic Association, Student Council, drama and just about anything else we wanted. Since we lived seven miles from our school, my Mom did a heck of a lot of driving for our after school activities. In her own way she was still encouraging our play with this effort. I needed to play so much, all the time, that despite all these activities I still had energy when I got home. To satisfy that always present need to play I spent several of my teenage years teaching myself how to play the piano. I am by no means a virtuoso, but I can play well enough for my own entertainment and the amusement of others at holiday gatherings.

One person told me that she had a similar high school experience, but was shocked and is still shocked by how it all dropped off <u>after</u> high school. In her large college there were literally thousands of people vying for the few slots in the chorus or band or sports teams. Recreational sports were limited for those who didn't make the teams. The disconnected nature of the college and campus made playing less likely to happen. Most likely the only time the students were getting to play was at a weekend party. I have begun to wonder in recent years why university and college curriculums are not as devoted to encouraging healthy play as they are educating. Why do we sign up for "courses" but not for things that effect the rest of our lives?

I watch my own college-age son search for companions to go snowboarding or hiking in the mountains, and come up empty-handed. Many are already working full-time in jobs while going to school and have little time for play. We need to look at this "work ethic" we are so worried about instilling in our children and ask ourselves why we are not equally concerned about their ability to play. Sure, I believe my children should work and study, but I also believe they should know how to enjoy a beautiful summer day or a snowy night and get some perspective about the difficulties they will encounter in life through relaxing, playful experiences.

The value of play as we progress through the teen years is gravely underrated, and to some a potential key to lessening the violence and unease that accompany these years. Dr. Stewart Brown, from the Institute for Play in California has devoted his life to studying the correlation between the individual's lack of play in childhood and their societal problems as adults. His first major foray into this area was after a shooting on the University of Texas campus. The lack of play in the history of the shooter is a factor that was studied to determine how this violence occurred. A rather sobering thought as we look at putting play in our lives. But, on a level closer to home, do we not feel more anger, weariness and pain when we have not played in a long time?

Another place from which messages about play come into our lives are comments from those we love. Even as adults we have a propensity to absorb the feedback of those around us, very often our loved ones. Sheila told me that she played heartily right into her adulthood, until her daughters became teenagers and told her that she was an embarrassment to them. Now this is the only time in history when a mother listened to her teenage daughters, but listen she did and she stopped playing. Women tell me that after they were married there was a sense that they could not be as playful as they were when single. They often curb the fun and silly stuff not to embarrass their spouses.

One of the most common things that women do is stop dancing. There is an old joke that men only dance to get married and then they stop. Not true for many men, but most. But does that mean that women have to stop too? Women have a free-spirited way of hearing a song and starting to wiggle and jiggle and move. Cooking to oldies, cleaning to rock and roll, maybe bathing to opera or washing the dog to a good old country and western tune. They used to do it. Remember those teen years when play was so sparse? Music was always there. Why do women stop dancing? What is the message? Men don't usually walk in the room and say "honey stop that, you look stupid," even if they do think it. They are sensitive to our silliness; many even love that about us. So why do we stop? I found myself dancing the other day while cooking dinner and the song "Shout" came on. I realized that I had all the curtains open and was providing quite the show for the neighbors. But you know what? I bet they were smiling and so was I. I was also totally refreshed after working very hard that day and I had a great evening by those few moments of pure pleasure. I was still smiling about my "dancecapade" when I fell asleep. Dancecapade is not in the dictionary so don't look it up. It is my word combining dance and an escapade!

In looking at yourself and your play history you will have to think carefully about the time where play changed for you. It either became less, very different or possibly non-existent. It is a fact that we have to grow up. It is a fact that we will have responsibilities. It is also a fact that it is not necessary for play to stop, change or diminish if we don't want it to.

6

Here Comes Life, Responsibility And The Kids – Look Out!

We have passed through our playful childhoods, matured through adolescence, finished high school and maybe college. We are off to work, marry and have children.

It has been an interesting study to look at people who are on this threshold. Many young single women in their twenties are very actively skiing, playing on softball or volleyball teams, biking, hiking, or into a hobby that makes their heart sing. Amazingly though, just as many are not. They are working very hard at jobs that require long hours and have little or no time for play. When they are not working, they are catching up on laundry and other chores and find that their down time maybe a club or party with friends, or during the week, watching television. Sadly, many feel that this is time to "pay their dues" in order to get a promotion or advance in their field. They are delaying play for a time when they are more established in their careers, making more money and in a more secure position with their company.

One of these women is someone who helped me along when I began my new business, Playmore. I'll never forget our first encounter, because when she heard what I did for a living she exclaimed, "oh no, I can't work on your project, I NEVER play." Over a period of six months she not only worked on my project, but many others for her employer. Her hours were long, her work hard and the experience invaluable. What happened next is the real story however. One day I put in a call to change something we were working on and she informed me that I would be getting a new account representative because she was leaving the company. She was planning to move and, for the next two months before her move was planning to take some time off and PLAY. There is no doubt in my mind that this woman was burned out, tired and missing the fun in her life. What is so amazing is that we do one thing—work—to the exclusion of the other thing—play. Play sneaks up on us and demands to come back into our lives. It would be a lot easier though, if we did not have to quit our jobs, move and take off months at a time to get our play going again.

What do our jobs do to us that make it so difficult to play? As we saw in the above example, there is the effort to get established. Look at any new college professor who has a job description that says you will teach, research, and publish if you want tenure. How about a resident or intern? Those who are new in the law profession expect long hard hours and work to become established. If one is beginning in management or maybe real estate there is some serious work to do to get going. It is a time of learning and applying ourselves, but does it have to be done to the exclusion of play? Some will say, there are not enough hours to do the work and have the play. I disagree. We can find time to play if we want it bad enough and believe it has value. Therein lies the purpose for this book and my work. Play does have value, just as work does. Only by giving yourself the gift of play in your life can you have the perspective you need about the hard work you undertake in your job.

In the past year I have interviewed three female executives in their forties. They were leaving very powerful positions with major U.S. corporations and going off to play for a while. The years of work, family and responsibility had taken their toll and it was time to put the play back. All three are planning to make their next jobs something that will allow more playfulness in their lives.

The CEO of a large corporation is known for his bicycle forays along the Jersey shore on Sunday mornings in the summer. One of the wealthiest men in the world is an avid marathoner. Look for him in Paris or New York, right next to the guy next door. I also know that he likes to hunt, fish, play golf and ride horses. Now you may say he has the time and the money. But knowing his busy schedule, what is important to note here is that he makes the time to do something that does not cost a lot of money.

My son is in the process of starting his own business. We had the typical talk of " if you work for yourself you will work ten times harder than with a company with regular hours." The difference is that his work is his play. He is taking the fun and the joy of a hobby and turning it into something that will generate income for him and give him a livelihood. He will work very hard, but he knows how to stop every now and then and play really hard. That may mean a day on the slopes or a hearty game of basketball with his friends, but he will take the time to re-energize through play.

One of the things we have to examine very carefully as careers, marriage and children fill our lives is whether we keep honoring the play that we need in our lives. The alternative is to say we are too busy, and that it is not important in the overall scheme of things. It is the thing we will let go to have enough time to get everything else done. We justify this decision by saying things like "my work is my play, my husband and I go to the movies on the weekend, I play with the children," and so on. Sure these are playful activities and what has been said may be true, but what is missing is the "Heart Play" that truly is yours alone. It not only relaxes you but causes you to become more comfortable with everything else that is going on in your life, even a very difficult job, or a house full of children and a traveling spouse.

Our lives most certainly change as we grow up and have more responsibilities. A new spouse is going to garner our attention. We will have to and want to do certain things with them and enjoy their company. This will take some of our free time away.

When you have a baby or two or three, things can get a little hectic. Maybe you have a blended family that involves shuttling kids between homes and events, adding even more chaos to the situation. All of these are legitimate uses of the time we have, but we need to look at them. We could be better at all of this by being true to ourselves and playing once in a while.

I know a stay-at-home Mom of three lovely children. They are busy as bees with swimming, soccer, baseball, piano lessons, church activities, school, craft classes and so on. Mom has wonderful homemaking skills, craft pursuits, but she is now searching for her "Heart Play." She had recently tried a golf lesson, because she wanted to go with her husband sometimes. She participates in many neighborhood activities, as she is both creative and hard working. She likes the social aspects of meeting and talking with people. She had lost her <u>own</u> play at this busy time in her life. While her household and children's activities are fun, she is really searching for something that will make her heart sing.

Too often as we fill our lives with the wonderful things that come from responsibilities, we lose a little bit of who we really are and the play that is uniquely ours. When we are not in touch with this "Heart play" we are at a loss to regenerate and re-energize ourselves. We feel more worn out and not quite as happy and carefree as when we were kids because the playfulness is not there. Without this playfulness we can't have the same unbridled, fresh look at the world we had when we were kids. Losing this childlike quality makes the world a little harsher and harder than it has to be. Remember what it felt like to greet the day knowing you would play with whatever came your way?

Just because we have taken on careers/jobs, partners and children it does not mean we have to give up our play. If you have done this, even a little bit, try a new attitude tomorrow. When you get up and step out the door, for work, to transport kids, to get chores done, ask yourself how you can take what comes your way today and make it play?

My friend Ann awoke a few Saturdays ago to face repainting a picnic table. Instead of this being a chore, she drafted her whole family to turn the table into a work of art. After painting the entire thing white, she then painted flower stems all over the table and her family created flowers at the end of each stem. They not only used paint, but glitter and glue and whatever they could find. Ann's play is painting, not little pictures, but big things that make a statement and create an impression. I am always impressed that she can find another wall, a table or the side of a barn to play on. She is also a chef, and someday you will probably go to her restaurant and get to paint with her, too.

There is the possibility that some of our play dreams need to be put on hold through childrearing years or a difficult time in our careers, but it is not necessary for us to forget about our play. I know people who carry around pictures or talk all the time about their play, even when they can't do it at the moment. By keeping our play in the front of our minds, it encourages us to make it through the rough spots and then get to it when the time is finally right. Just be sure you don't wait too long or nature may conspire against your dreams. I have a habit of clipping pictures of places I want to go and things I want to do and glancing at them when I am working long hours. It lightens my load and makes me even more determined to finish up and get to play.

7

Gender Differences — Do Men And Women Really Play Differently?

I have had a great time interviewing both men and women for this book. The women's stories have been everything from sad to exciting. The men's stories have been consistent. They love to play, they honor play, and play is without a doubt absolutely sacred to them. Even Warren Buffet and Bill Gates get together for bridge tournaments. There is barely a week in most men's lives where they do not interject some form of play; unless that week takes them out of town for work. Even then they are apt to find a way to interject play.

I was calling my husband once when he was traveling and had to leave a voice message on his phone. Since he worked long hours on the road and had many late nights and early mornings I did not think much of it when I got the voice mail in the middle of the day. He called me back later to tell me he was at the new Woody Allen movie for a few hours. Play in the middle of the day! I was shocked. Why should I be? Men are excellent at integrating work and play. With his long hours and crazy schedule, good for him for taking a little time to play.

Business deals on the golf course or in the clubhouse are not uncommon. Every baseball stadium in America is filled with businessmen every time there is an afternoon game. Cell phones, suits, hot dogs and baseball. Playing. Of course I began to look for the logical female correlation to afternoon baseball. Shopping with the girls? Three-hour lunch and gab session. Not very likely. The women are working! Many women told me when I asked that they would probably get fired if they tried. Does this make the world unfair? Do men have it better, again? Not really. They have just learned how to do some things in the world of play that we now need to learn too.

Men have shown through their stories that they are players, all the time. Always were and always will be. We all grew up with the expression, "you can tell the men from the boys by the size of their toys." I don't think it is just the size, but the number, the variety and the consistency of them in men's lives.

Drive by a high school or college and you will see clusters of young men playing hacky sack, Frisbee, touch football, of a quick game of baseball. They need only the break from school and they are at it. Adult men play golf, climb mountains, have regular tennis dates, sail boats, tinker with cars, ride motorcycles, belong to a biking club, or bike on their own. Women do these things too, but there are nowhere near as many of them indulging in these types of play. I recently took up running (at my age that is quite the undertaking). When I went to a "runner's" store for shoes I was the only female customer. I didn't ask, but on a ratio basis what do you think the numbers look like of men to women runners? Even with our numbers increasing it will probably be a two to one ratio.

Okay so the women are playing at other things. Sewing? Knitting? Cooking? Painting or sculpting? Reading? Let us see.

On a typical Saturday morning in America the alarm is usually ignored, unless the kids have to be at a school or sporting event. When the family does rise, there is a lazy breakfast for some and the work begins for others. Still others are out the door to a "play date." You know, tee time for golf, tennis match, car show, etc. Most women have an agenda for the day. Laundry, grocery shopping, cleaning, errands, yard or garden work, bills to be paid, paperwork from the week's mail, phone calls to family, so on and so on.

Men like to wake up on Saturday and play. Sure they know the lawn needs to be mowed and they may even do it before they play, but then they play.

Now back to our woman. She is still going through this mental list of things that need to be done which is now expanded to getting ready for a church or community event, possibly preparing a meal for guests over the weekend and finding a new chair for the living room have been added to the list. Meanwhile, back at man camp, he has already finished 18 holes and is at the 19th having a sandwich and a beer. Good guy that he is he heads home to help. When he comes through the door he flicks on the TV to catch the scores of the afternoon games and then heads off to do a chore or two. Poking his head in every now and then to keep up with the games. Maybe even sitting a spell to watch a close one. (This has always been affectionately referred to as the *Dagwood* Syndrome thanks to the comic strip).

Our Saturday woman is heading home now with the evening meal preparations in the car and planning on how she will shower, cook, and present all this before the guests arrive.

During an enjoyable dinner with friends that evening the subjects of golf scores, children, finding a good plumber and the price of gas are likely topics. They are easy, on our minds, and neutral.

Now much has been accomplished by both the man and the woman in this day, but if you were to keep score on the time that was play for each, the man easily outscores the woman. By the way, she might just stay up after the guests have left to see if she can solve world peace or starvation. Women are very responsible people.

Note this cute piece that recently made the rounds on the Internet, author unknown:

Why I Love My Mom....

Mom and Dad were watching TV when Mom said, "I'm tired, and it's getting late. I think I'll go to bed."

She went to the kitchen to make sandwiches for the next day's lunches, rinsed out the popcorn bowls, took meat out of the freezer for supper the following evening, checked the cereal box levels, filled the sugar container, put spoons and bowls on the table and started the coffee pot for brewing the next morning. She then put some wet clothes in the dryer, put a load of clothes in the wash, ironed a shirt and secured a loose button. She picked up the game pieces left on the table and put them back in the drawer. She watered the plants, emptied a wastebasket and hung up a towel to dry. She yawned and stretched and headed for the bedroom. She stopped by the desk and wrote a note to the teacher, counted out some cash for the field trip, and pulled a textbook out from hiding under a chair. She signed a birthday card for a friend, addressed and stamped the envelope and wrote a quick note for the grocery store. She put both near her purse.

Mom then washed her face, put on moisturizer, brushed and flossed her teeth and trimmed her nails.

Dad called out, " I thought you were going to bed?"

"I'm on my way," she said. She put some water into the dog's dish and called the cat in, then made sure the doors were locked. She looked in on each of the kids and turned out a bedside lamp, hung up a shirt, threw some dirty socks in the hamper, and had a brief conversation with the one still up doing homework. In her own room she set the alarm, laid out clothing for the next day, straightened up the shoe rack. She added three things to her list of things to do for tomorrow.

About that time, Dad turned off the TV and announced to no one in particular, "I'm going to bed."

And he did...without another thought.

What does this little story tell us? More importantly, why did it get passed around on the Internet so much?

Am I exaggerating here a little? Sure I am, maybe I am exaggerating a lot. But let's look at some of the real life stories that men told me and you be the judge.

Jim is a successful health care professional. He works hard all week and is anxious to enjoy his play and his children on the weekends. One morning he came bouncing down stairs with the kids ready to take off for a day of adventure and fun with the kids. One of their passions is remote-control sailboats and the day was perfect to be out doing just that.

As he rounded the corner to the living area of the house he ran into his wife standing on a stepladder with glued wallpaper ready to be hung. Jim said he actually did think about staying home and helping for a minute or two, but alas the "play plans" were made and he and the children headed out for a fun-filled day. Now we can all only hope that Jim's wife's idea of play was to hang wallpaper so she had an equally good day.

In analyzing this story do we think of Jim as a bad guy for not helping his wife? Absolutely not. Jim has a life and a need to play that is as important as anything else that needs to be done, including hanging wallpaper. How about Jim's wife? Maybe this was fun and play for her. If it wasn't we should not feel sorry for her. We choose the things we do and we are only responsible for ourselves. If she wanted to play at something other than hanging wallpaper she could do so. So what is the purpose of this story? The purpose is to point out that play is a choice. There are always chores and they will get done, but when, to what extent, and how frequently is a choice.

A colleague of mine and her husband have an agreement that they will not do chores on the weekend and "play" instead. She is very unhappy with this because she is a perfectionist and desperately wants everything in her home to be picture perfect. Her "play" days with him can be somewhat agonizing for her because all she can do is focus on what she wants to be doing at home. This is a real play dilemma.

Her desire to "work" on her house may actually have play in it, even if it looks like work to the rest of the world. Americans just about fell over when President George Bush's wife Laura announced that her way of relaxing was to "clean house." I bet the housekeepers in the White House were happy to hear they were getting more help! Don't ridicule her for this. Admire her for knowing what makes her heart sing and going for it, even if the rest of the world thinks it is dumb.

Miles is a top business executive in a $100 million company. He reports to the CEO and is on call twenty-four hours a day because of his job description. One time I noticed Miles missing from a meeting and Miles explained to me later that he had a tennis doubles date during that time. When I inquired how he got excused when everyone else had to come, he told me that he said he needed to be elsewhere and he was. No excuses, he had a "play date" and he would not break it. Did he say he was playing tennis? No, but he didn't work either and if the implication was that he was off working on something else, so be it.

I have heard an unsubstantiated rumor that a major executive left his position recently when he was forced to work during trick or treat time on Halloween. He claimed he would never do that again and walked out of the company. He missed a play date and it was important to him. I hope the rumor is true. Because playing with our kids is even more important than play for ourselves.

Millie is a happily married stepmother of three beautiful girls. They are living with her and her husband most of the time and Millie enjoys them enormously. They shop, talk and grow together. When I met Millie to talk about her playtime an interesting story developed. Millie's husband is a play devotee. He skis a lot on the weekends, he rock climbs once a week, weather permitting, and he belongs to a once a week in-line skate group. When I asked Millie if she participated in these things she explained that she was neither a climber nor a skater, and she went skiing reluctantly on the weekends, but it put her behind in household matters. Millie is now learning to play more and looking at what her "Heart Play" is and how to get the time in her life to do the things she loves. Her spouse has what he loves; now it is her turn. He is not doing anything that isn't normal and natural for him or that he should forsake for her. This is her choice and her journey.

David was an interesting interview. At one time David worked with a firm that had a very double standard built into it for men's play and women's play. The standard was very simple; the men were allowed to play together at work, during work and after work. The women were not. I could not believe my ears. This is the twenty-first century and I was sure that this was an exaggeration. Alas, he quickly outlined three events in the past week that had occurred and all were done with the exclusion of the women in the group.

That was just the way things were. Okay, so now even when women want to play they are not welcome? Is this a problem? I don't think so. I friend of mine told me that she watched this occur in her company and decided to do something about it. One of the men's favorite "play events" was a smoker. Whiskey, cards and cigars, mixed with lots of laughter. When she organized just such an event at her home, and only invited the women, she was immediately challenged by her boss to explain her actions. She explained that she thought the women might like to have some fun too. Although she does not have plans to become a cigar smoker or even drink whiskey and play cards, she does intend to play with her colleagues and will work hard to have play in her life. She knows the secret.

What is the secret here? Men are staying and enjoying their work as they go into their forties and fifties because they have play in their lives. The women are burning out, even "crisping out" because they are exhausted. Exhausted mentally, physically and spiritually they want their lives back. I participated on a panel where CEO's were asking what they can do to keep their female employees, because they were bailing out the doors. Many were concerned about meeting affirmative action goals or complaints from shareholders, but most really wanted to know how to keep the talent that these women brought to their companies. When the women were leaving they were not going to a competitor, they were starting their own businesses or working in new professions. The reason for these career changes is that the new work or business offered them an opportunity to "play." Maybe the business is even their play. I know mine is, and I have many friends starting to do the same thing.

One of my relatives opened a health spa with all treatments being done by former nurses. Has anyone heard about the nursing shortage in our hospitals? Ironically when I initially went to a major hospital chain to see if we could do some "play" training with their nurses to balance their work with play, I was treated politely, but they dismissed the idea because they were too busy looking for other solutions to their problems. Recently there has been a lot more interest and I now speak to nursing groups on a regular basis, as hospital systems recognize the need for balance in what can be a difficult profession.

A very good friend of mine had her career initially in women's athletics, at the college level. She provided me with some enlightening accounts of how women were treated and thought of historically in play, which emphasizes the differences again between men and women. She spoke about the "mythology" that accompanies women so often when they grow up, such as being excused from gym class because the woman was having her period. This gave the impression to everyone, including the woman being excused, that she was somehow not as physically able to do things because she was a woman.

Now I do not dispute the real physical differences of men and women. We know that men can be faster and stronger than women. Men have their centers of balance in their shoulders, which gives them extra strength. Women on the other hand have their center of balance in their hips. Now what is interesting about this difference is that a man on the balance beam is not nearly as exciting to watch as a woman. With that high center of gravity the balance beam is not an easy sport for men. Whereas the men on the rings usually can outperform the women using their natural upper body strength. Again and again my friend told stories of how women have been "contaminated" by the mythology of physical limitation. So women don't do the rings, they can do the balance beam. So women don't normally wrestle for the same reason. My friend's daughter proved that they could if they are determined enough. She was the only woman on her high school wrestling squad and while not a champion she had her share of wins.

We all know how this goes. As my friend says, it all started with Herbert Hoover's wife who personified what a "lady" did. I think it was there long before that, but it is a myth that has gone on way too long. Remember when women went into seclusion and didn't do much during pregnancy? Today we see them running down the street and pushing another kid in the stroller, while pregnant with the second. Doctors all over agree that healthy exercise during pregnancy does wonders for mother and child.

I think the thing my friend pointed out that really hit home is that since men are usually faster and stronger than women they are naturally more successful in "men's play." This in turn creates a message to women that they are not as physically competent and quite often this becomes a self-fulfilling prophecy. One story that I got from Brandi was that she loved gymnastics in high school, but could not find an equivalent when she moved on into her twenties. Her comment was that she wished she had played volleyball or softball, because her friends were still able to do those things after high school and college. I think we need to become committed to what are the equivalents when we run into something like this. Possibly we have a whole new field of endeavors in finding ways to continue our high school sports into our adult lives. Men have been doing this for years. My first brother-in-law used to get up at four o'clock in the morning to go and play hockey with his friends before they showered and shaved for a business day and suits.

Women are flocking to the gyms and health clubs, but the "workouts" are quite often solitary and not as much play as just exercise. The difference with the hockey game is that it is both play and exercise. Again, women do not necessarily like competitive play as much as men, so what would really be fun? Jazzercise hit the scene big years ago because it combined dancing (remember that women love to dance) and exercise. They were having fun. Now we see women in all sorts of new and adventuresome things that combine play and exercise.

I cannot leave this topic of the mythology of the physical differences between men and women without telling the story of the first women's athletics. First of all, not so many years ago it was actually a rule that women were FORBIDDEN from receiving athletic scholarships. This was done because of a belief that it was a detriment to a women's femininity to play sports, whereas it affirmed a man's masculinity to engage in sports. I know that this is history, but I could not help but notice a few recent movies where this stereotype was played out yet again. You know, the man playing the hero, fighting all the fights and the women in the background. Now thank you *Charlie's Angels* and few other similar shows that change this, but we still have a lot of women waiting to be saved by Mel Gibson or Harrison Ford.

Another great story that forms our history in getting into sports is the story of the "femguard." This is a protective device that was worn by women basketball players when they first started playing on college teams. Again, there was this mythology that any physical contact to the breast would cause cancer. I can only picture a team of women with their "chest coverings", running up and down the court. Quite the spectacle, to say nothing of the inconvenience and the weight.

I have highlighted the gender differences in play because as we look to put more play in our lives, we need role models, we need to know the truth, and we need to know that it can be done. Most men are very good at play. They can role model doing chores AFTER WE PLAY. They can role model a less fancy meal or eating out with friends to avoid overdoing the entertainment. They can role model that you can take a few hours during the day and take care of your playful self and that your employer can see the value in that. It is time for it to stop being so hard for women to be playful in all parts of their lives. I am not talking about walking out for two hours of play everyday or even dancing in the aisles, but having simple joy that comes with simple play, like men are doing more than we know. (Ever heard of a football pool in the office?)

Carol told me that when she was not allowed to bring play into her work in any way, shape or form, and I mean not even cartoons, she quit her job. She told me that play is so important to her that she will eat macaroni while she finds a place that will honor her need to have a playful life. Carol is a quiet, unassuming and wonderful woman who will work harder than anyone. Why anyone ever let her leave his or her company is beyond me. What was even scarier about this story was the fact that the person who would not allow any playfulness in the workplace was also a woman.

Sure there are exceptions to the concept that all men play well. Some men are struggling as women are to find their "Heart Play." I hope they will join us on our journey so everyone is playing in the end!

8
What In My Heart
I Know To Be True
About Play

As we look at life each day there are many components to the decisions we make and eventually do with the hours that lie ahead. I am drawn to the planning, scheduling, preparing, meeting, mentoring, coaching, counseling, and general busyness to decide how, what, where, when, why and who on every issue that comes along. Now I admit that there are good reasons to plan and prepare, but I wonder what would happen if there were just a little less preparation and a little more "go with the flow." The reason for this topic is that play is not so easily planned for, prepared for, and scheduled as you would like to think. It is something that comes from deep within your heart and you know instinctually when you get to it that it is right.

As we have discussed before there is the sense of "free play" when we watch children. When a young child is brought into a room, or a forest clearing, their eyes light upon something and off they go to explore. It may hold their interest or it may not. When it does not, they simply cast it aside and move on to the next thing. They do not feel committed to what they started and will not continue to play with it if it does not satisfy their hearts. Children have very little to go by in this life so they go by their instinct or what feels good to them. They follow their hearts endlessly. They make no judgments about what feels good or bad, they just feel those things and move on or stay, as it feels best.

We need to have this freedom of discovery built very deep into our being and allow the good and the bad to come along. We need to allow ourselves to make mistakes in finding our "Heart Play" and cast aside that which is not comfortable or fun for us and look further inside ourselves to find the play that gives us life.

When I began this journey to find my "Heart Play" many years ago one of the first things I did was make a list of all the adventures and fun things I would do to play more. This list should be framed in my gallery of great mistakes. (A gallery that has many other things in it if you have lived a full and rich life). On this list were such things as go to the local amusement park, skydive, and take exercise classes. Well, let us look at this list from my heart perspective, which I eventually did. First of all I hate crowds, not dislike, hate crowds. I am a person who likes her space and going to a crowded amusement park would not be my idea of fun. Next I realized that I have always disliked heights. Now very few of the good amusement park rides are on the ground. What was I thinking? Whoa, let's see skydiving is next. This for the woman who does not like heights? Get a grip! Finally the exercise classes. I cannot honestly say that I have ever enjoyed an exercise class in my life, and we are talking starting with gym class in elementary school. Not because they are not good, or well done or have good teachers, because they can and do have all of those things. But I like to exercise alone or with one other person, I always have and I always will.

So the question is why did these things make my list? Because I was totally and completely incapable of knowing or understanding what play meant to me.

With this simple little exercise I had broken the first rule of playing. I had tried to plan it. I made a list. I pondered it. I planned what I thought I SHOULD play. None of these are the right way to go about this process and none of these would have brought the right play into my life.

Like a child we must look at this world as one huge toy store, sand box, open field. We must look into our lives and see the absolutely unlimited possibilities for play and then let them slowly come to us with the opening of our spirit to play.

In the pursuit of this new, playful you, the first step on the journey will involve a resolve that you really want play in your life. Can you honestly say that you would do anything to play again like a child? Yes, proceed with glee. No? Think about what is holding you back. Do you have a sense that it is selfish to play? That you do not have the time? That it is a waste of time? If any of these doubts linger in your mind go back and reread "Why We Need To Play" Chapter Three more time. This is YOUR LIFE! It is the only one you will get that we know of, so it should be lived to the fullest. It also does not wait for the kids to grow up, work to slow down, the spouse to stop traveling so much, the sun to shine, or the rainbows to appear. YOUR LIFE DOES NOT WAIT FOR ANYONE BUT YOU TO GET ON BOARD AND START HAVING JOY.

Resolve can be managed in a variety of ways. You need to sit down with a piece of paper that will remain in your possession forever, so choose it carefully. It needs to be a journal page if you journal, or a full-page sign or a small note that goes in a special box. One way or the other, it must be a part of your life from this point forward. Why? Because anything really important that you have done in your life has had a contract with your signature on it to guarantee its provisions. When you got married you got a license and signed it. When you bought a house, a car, a boat, you signed a contract. When you went to college you applied for admission and signed an application. When you opened your bank account you signed an agreement. When you opened a charge account you signed an agreement. See how many agreements with many, many other people you have? Now it is time to sign an agreement with yourself.

This agreement has to contain the following elements. First, it must start with an "I" statement. I will, I shall, I promise, I guarantee, whatever word most aptly fits you and what your level of commitment is to this process is the beginning. Remember the Declaration of Independence, "We the people...."

Next comes the statement that you really, really, really want to have more joy in your life. Notice that we did not start with the play statement. Because the play is really only a means to an end. We want JOY. We want Wealth. We want Health. These are the statements you need to make to begin your agreement. Write out what you want for joy. Describe what that looks like to the people around you. For example, people will always see me smiling. My eyes will shine. My skin will glow. My step will be lighter. I will walk with my eyes up to the sky. Describe how it will feel to you. I will wake up happy. I will know that my day will be full of joy and many great surprises. I know that I will be able to feel good even when things are tough. I know that my heart will beat slowly and strong with the peace that I get from my joy. Describe every conceivable good thing that you could feel because of this new joy that you have found.

I had the pleasure of meeting several of the most joyful humans to ever walk this planet when I went to Hawaii for a spiritual retreat. This group of women was amazing. They had lives where they demanded that joy be a part of everything they did. I watched them deal with everything from the frustration of finding a parking space to the sudden ill health of one of their parents with joy and with very positive and wonderful outcomes. Joy was literally a force that was wrapped around each one of them and when you got near their smile, their laughter, their unconditional love for those around them made you feel like a million dollars, just to be in their presence! Powerful stuff, joy. What will you look and feel like?

Next go into how you will look to others with your newfound wealth. A mountain sage once told me that you really cannot tell a wealthy person when you see them. They look, well, like everyone else. Some wealthy people do have an arrogance about their wealth. Is that what you want to look like? Think carefully about how you would like to look with your newfound wealth and describe it. Now write about how you will feel with your newfound wealth. Such as, I will have a sense of peace about me when it comes to making financial decisions. I will no longer feel afraid when it is time to pay the bills. I will no longer worry about where and how I will pay for impending financial needs. I will be comfortable with the money I have! The mountain sage that I referred to earlier told me that he had enormous wealth because he lived in a beautiful mountain town, had good work, and the opportunity to leave the small town frequently to either go to the big city or even further into the country. He had the love of his partner, children, parents, brothers and sisters. He absolutely revels in the wildlife that lives outside his door. He is also not even close to being a millionaire, but boy does he exude wealth.

Now let us make a statement about our health. First of all, what does it look like to others? Do we walk tall and straight? Are our eyes clear and smiling? Do we breathe slowly and easily? Are we in shape to do the things we like to do without strain? Next describe how healthy you will feel. What does really good health feel like to you? When you wake up in the morning what does health feel like to you? For me, it was to be free of terrible hip joint pain when I woke up after a night's sleep. As I embarked on my play journey it really wasn't on my mind that I get rid of the pain in my hips. But as I played I began to walk straighter and taller and soon the hip joints were back where they should have been and the pain went away! Weird, but true. Play has some miraculous health benefits besides the obvious. What is it in your health that it is time to get rid of? Alan Cohen tells the story of a 17-year-old boy named Edward who had cancer and was struggling with a protracted regimen of chemotherapy. One day he found out that the Grateful Dead were playing at the same time he was scheduled for his chemotherapy session. He chose to go to the concert and soon after his condition was reversed and he has been cancer free for several years now. His statement about his choice tells it all, "I believe that it was my choice to be kind to myself that made all the difference."

Being kind to ourselves is what play is all about. You have now started the process by giving yourself a contract to sign that indicates what you want from play in the areas of joy, wealth and health. You now need to finish this contract with a statement about finding your play that you feel you can live up to. In other words you are the one who is doing this. You are the one on a play journey and only you can make a statement about what you are going to do.

If this were a legal contract it would have certain provisions that enforce what needs to occur. If you are truly committed to play in your life you will have to find a way to state what it is you are willing to do to get it. For example, my statement was that I will do anything to get play back into my life, and I meant it. What are the activities that you will undertake to get this play? Will you read about it? Will you write down your thoughts on what might be fun? Will you make phone calls to find out about classes or adventures? Will you talk to friends about your ideas and see if they can add to them? Will you join a playgroup? Will you MAKE THE TIME to do any or all of these things and more? (See a later chapter for how to find the time; don't worry about where it will come from just now.)

Now read your statement back to yourself. Is it really you? Is it what you think you want today, but maybe a little unsure? What is the reason you want to do this primarily? Is that reflected somewhere in here? Give yourself a huge gift when you are through with this statement. Find a symbol of some type to wear or leave out in an obvious place that will remind you of this commitment. Sometimes these symbols are as simple as something that has been stored away, like a piece of jewelry that you have not worn in a long time. You bring it out and wear it again while you start this process. Or you could get a new piece of jewelry. If jewelry is not for you, you could find a picture of you as a playful child and put it on your bathroom mirror or nightstand. Others like simple things like a shiny rock or a feather. Whatever you choose make sure it is YOU.

When we look at the lives of adult women there is an interesting phenomenon going on. It is lives that are filled with so much and so many interactions and people and places and things and so little true "Heart Play." One reason is the simple lack of time, but the larger reason is we lost what play is to us. Our romance with play wanes as we age, and I mean age as being over 21. When we moved from being little girls to young women we found love, work, responsibility and sleep deprivation to be our major life components. Looking at these one by one we found love through a partner or good friends or family. We found our life's work whether that is a career outside the home or staying at home to raise children. We found responsibility in caring for ourselves, those we love, and the world at large. We also found that these things take up a major part of the day and leave little time for outside pursuits. When we decide to play we decide to risk. We are going to disturb the apple cart of life and take some time to do something we truly love. When we agree to take this risk we are then going to stimulate a new romance with life. This new romance is then going to blossom and grow until we see all of the fundamental components of our life differently. We will question our "love" for some people, places and things and maybe re-categorize them into things that we "like" and spend a little less time with them. I heard a great example of this with one woman, who while on her play discovery journey found out that she "liked" skiing, but didn't love it like she thought. What had truly drawn her to the sport was the opportunity to do something with her husband. She hasn't given up skiing and in fact still goes just as much, but now she sees it for what it is, a means to an end, being with a wonderful, loving spouse and her day is enjoyed accordingly. Whether she skis well or not is a moot point while she revels in the pleasure of the company she is in. She is also now making time for her true "Heart Play." So she has a double dose of fun and play in her life.

9

What Does "Heart Play" Feel Like? How Will I Know?

Now here is an interesting thought. When we are really playing can we actually feel the difference? Yes, we can. "Heart Play" gives us a variety of feelings, and when you get there you know you are really playing the way you were meant to play. Let's look at this feeling by once again seeing how children play and what they feel when they play.

Total Abandonment

When a young child plays there are several things that you can observe right away. First, they are completely abandoned to their play, nothing else in the world matters. This is the only place they want to be at that time and they are completely abandoned to it. They have no cares, no worries, they are not too hot, not too cold, they are not too high, not too low, you know what I mean, a place that lacks stress, pain, disease, ill ease. What a great place to be!

No Worry

The second thing you will notice is that they feel no worry. They may fret over the play, but they do not fret over life. The feeling of play does not allow worry to come into it, even if there are great worries out there to be dealt with later. Worrying is not allowed in "Heart Play." A child may often cope with very difficult life situations by going out to play. I loved the movie, <u>Billy Elliot</u>, where Billy's father and brother are out on a miner's strike while their home life is filled with stress and pain. To "cope" with this Billy would dance. Not just a little dance, but a dance that totally consumed him, and felt "like electricity is pouring through me." In the midst of what would be great worry and pain, for a few moments there was none. Billy was free to FEEL from head to toe through his dance.

Joy

When we begin to find our "Heart Play," one of the things that will measure whether we have found it or not will be the feeling of joy. Joy is that wonderfully mysterious feeling that warms our souls, puts an involuntary smile on our faces and causes the heart to pump our blood in a way that nourishes our body. Joy is that feeling of, "I wish this moment would last forever," "I will keep this moment in my heart forever." (If you are having trouble recalling true joy in your life then you can easily recall a joyful moment to get into the spirit of what I am talking about.) When my first child was born, the joy as I lay in my hospital bed and held him can send shivers through my spine even today. When my second child was born there is an image of my husband holding him that does the same thing to me. I saw a sunrise this morning that would have had an artist running for their paints it was so magnificent. When we are in our "Heart Play" we will create joyful moments just like those from our past.

Clear Thinking

The next feeling that play brings into our being is that of clearing the cobwebs from our heads. Play has the ability to bring a feeling of clear-headedness to you that you may have only experienced before from a good night's rest or meditation. Good "Heart Play" allows our energy to flow to where we are the strongest and thus the brightest. It gives our brains and our memories a chance to operate at their most optimal level because we feel so good. The mud begins to move, the clouds clear away, the stars come out, the fog lifts, you know clarity, the one thing we wish we could have so much of the time when life is just so confusing. Watch a good sports team focus on their play and then watch them as they leave their field of play. One of the things you will notice is how attentive they are to what happens next to them. You will not see befuddlement, you will not see confusion, you will not see indecisiveness, **and you will see** clear-headed thinking at least in the short term. Once life and conversation and distractions occur some of this clear-headedness will go away. The fact is that even those few moments of being able to think clearly will allow your mind to formulate solutions to problems and concerns, or maybe to decide that they are not the problem you thought they were. Maybe in these moments of clear thinking you will feel the answer to a nagging problem. You may feel clear enough in your thoughts to create something new when you get back to your regular work and routine.

Energy

The next thing you will feel in your "Heart Play" is energy. Oh, could we not use more of that every day of the week! You have already probably used rest and exercise to increase your energy, so understanding how play can do this for you will be simple. You will feel more energy because just like in rest and exercise, you are giving your heart and head the opportunity to work in a place that is comfortable, warm and nourishing and all those good things. Play is an energy boost without the energy bar or energy drink. It is a boost from your heart that goes to your head and says, "bring it on, I'm ready."

Play takes energy too, but in a good way. When children play really hard they top off that play with a nap. Do you nap? Do you play hard enough to need a nap? Play moves energy around our bodies in such a way that the body will do much good work, nourish itself and then want to rest. For example, have you ever watched someone reading a book or doing a simple handcraft and then nod off? Well, you say they are just tired. Very true. But, their play puts them in a place to go to sleep and rest peacefully, as their body needs. Other times play is actually tiring. I love to hike in the wilderness near my mountain retreat. I then feel very energized to work. I then feel very inclined to a leisurely nap. My play, hiking, gives me energy, but it also gives me rest which is an energy restorative. Just working hard and getting tired does not give me the peaceful, restful sleep I need, but only a very fitful and uneven rest that is anything but restorative.

Curiosity

Play allows us to feel curious. Curiosity is not what killed the cat, it is what created great joy and glee for us as children. How often have you heard adults say that they love to be around children because they are so curious? They want to know why the sky is blue, they want to know why the grass is green, they want to know why birds fly and chickens don't since they both have wings. In our play we are allowed the opportunity to feel is curious again. A painter is curious about what would happen if they changed the colors this way or that, a hiker is curious about what is around that bend, a collector is curious about how the value of an item changes, a breeder is curious about trying a different mix. Curiosity is fun, because it leads us to new discoveries and visions of things we have not yet thought of. Einstein was curious, the pilgrims were even more curious. Curiosity also leads us to discover things about ourselves. When I decide to be curious and playful, I find things that amaze me. They amaze me because they point to how complex the world is and thus wondrously fascinating to explore, and they amaze me because I learn and learn and learn. For me, learning is always play.

Wonderment

Play opens our eyes to wonderment. We feel a sense of wonderment while deeply in our "Heart Play." It is a feeling that defies description. No matter how simple our play, sewing, painting a wall, planting, biking, our play has the companion of wonderment. Wonderment is that feeling Walt Disney was looking for when he created Disneyland. It was the feeling George Lucas was looking for when he created all the characters of *Star Wars*. Wonderment is that feeling we have when we "wonder" what will come next, who is behind that door, what does the next thing I am about to do look like, feel like, smell like, taste like. Wonderment is the feeling of light and energy. Play can bring that wonderment to our lives.

Pride

Play can be the door that opens to a world where we can feel pride. Pride in our ability, pride in our accomplishment, pride in our taking a chance. Pride is something that brings so much to us, yet we have been taught so often that it is not good. What is not good about being proud of a good job? What is not good about being proud of the effort we put into something? What is not good about being prideful when what we have done has made us feel better about ourselves? Not too long ago I was speaking with a friend about a major undertaking that she and about 150 other women took on, doing a mini marathon. She told me that one of the husbands kept asking why are you doing this? Finally, the day before the marathon she was able to look at him and say, "Because it makes us feel good about ourselves." She was very proud of the hard work she put into training. She had a wonderful time playing with the other women as they slogged their way through learning open water swimming, biking hills and vales and for many, running for the very first time. We use the words pride and proud for others all the time. "I was so proud of my son, my daughter, my husband." Do we say as frequently we are proud of ourselves? Is that being boastful or is it being real? When we are in our "Heart Play" we are doing something that we are proud of, proud of for ourselves. We aren't doing it to get others' affirmations, or even their approval. We are also not doing it to one-up anyone. We are playing for our hearts, to make them sing.

I observed a small child playing at my cabin one time, gathering sticks and rocks and making what appeared to be some type of structure. His pride in this structure was evident in every move he made throughout his play. Another stick here, a leaf there, a branch here, a rock tilted just so and the glow of pride around it all. It is so easy to be proud of our work; do we know how to be proud of our play?

Connection

Play gives us connection to the rest of the world and sometimes even to parts of ourselves. Life is so often a mumble jumble of things and people and places. It can actually begin to feel that we are disconnected from the things we truly love, from the people we really want to be with and from the places that nourish us. Play is one of the ways of feeling connected to many of these again.

A story I saw on television lately followed a group of elderly people who mostly lived alone, but all had a common hobby. They played cards at a club in Manhattan. While these very serious players were joyfully concentrating on the games they played they were also connecting. Some of the most interesting elements of this story were the coffees after the games were over, the lunches that went on before the games began, and the phone calls to chat in between the scheduled games. People connecting with people. If you have ever been to a horse race you will know that almost everyone at the fence is connecting with each other, (looking for tips), and maybe even trying to connect with the horses. Everywhere there is play there are people connecting. A friend of mine had all the girls on her daughter's soccer team make a scrapbook to mark the season and fill it with pictures, notes to each other, things they picked up along the way, and good wishes. In their play they found a way of connecting.

Sometimes play reconnects us with a thing, like a musical instrument that has been in storage or an old pair of tap shoes. Sometimes we reconnect with a place that had nourished us in the past, but because we stopped playing we lost the connection. One of the things that demonstrate this in a simple way is the swing set at the park. Maybe we push our kids, or grandkids, or other people's kids on the swings, but do we get on them? We experience not only reconnection with the swing, but also reconnection with being outdoors in the park and the feeling of flying through the air that swinging gives to us.

Playing connects us with what we really want in life, not just what is thrown at us each day.

Movement

Play evokes a feeling of moving through life instead of standing still. It gives us the momentum not to be stuck. Being stuck can mean a thousand different things. We are sometimes stuck in our thinking, in our daily routine, in a relationship, and sometimes we don't even know we are stuck! Play creates a sense of movement toward the things that please us, and from there we make choices about other things we like. Our lives will build on one thing to the next, with play leading the way. Without play we are doing what seems to be right, maybe what the media tells us is right, or maybe what our parents or spouses tell us is right. With play we are doing what feels really good to us, even if we move in the wrong direction sometimes.

I will never forget one of my birthdays when I ended up spending the day at a funeral for my Aunt Frances. In the evening we were all settled back at my parent's home and I was feeling so disconnected from reality and dealing with the loss of my Aunt, and a thousand other things. I took off to my bedroom to do some Tai Chi, which is one of my play activities that gives me the added benefit of stretching and relaxation. What it also does is create movement. The get up, get-out–of-the-chair type of movement. It changed everything about that day. I was moving within myself again, and when I returned downstairs I was able to socialize and spend a nice evening with all my family members.

Play that does not involve physical movement to a great degree still creates that movement in our mental energies. A jigsaw puzzle or drawing will create that movement in our systems that enhance everything about our lives.

Imagination

We can imagine all sorts of things when we play, and this imagining has been at the heart of our existence since we were able to think. Imagine being able to fly to the moon. Imagine living in that house. Imagine climbing that mountain. Imagine swimming in those perfect blue waters. Imagine creating something that tastes so wonderful. Imagine designing something so beautiful. Imagine the perfect companion.

Childhood is filled with this feeling of imagination. We imagined we were all sorts of things and it took us further and further into our play. We were queens and kings, we were detectives and warriors, we were the ultimate Moms and Dads, we were the ultimate sports champion, we won the

Miss America pageant, we won the Pulitzer prize, we won a gold medal. We imagined all of that and for some people it really happened.

In our play as adults we need to feel again what it is like to imagine. As in childhood, we did not necessarily become kings and queens and win all sorts of contests and awards, but we sure had a good time doing it. While we were playing we added this imaginative element to our play and had the feeling of winning, even when we didn't.

Since I dabble in music quite a bit I get to imagine. When I am on my clarinet I imagine being with a symphony. (Now you can even get symphonic CD accompaniment). There I am singing in my car and imagining myself on stage. Imagination is a feeling play brings that warms our hearts.

Relaxation

When we play we relax. This is so obvious and so simple that you tend to take this feeling for granted. Let's talk about how relaxed you get when you play. When you are playing your body, your mind, and your emotions are usually very tied up in what you are doing. In fact, should you be choosing a very challenging form of play, such as mountain climbing, it would look anything but relaxing to a casual bystander. However, when we are playing we are relaxing all these aspects of ourselves. Sure we are still putting out physical effort, but it is the kind of effort that feels good to the body. We are concentrating hard and really spinning those mental wheels to think about what we are working on in our play, but it is a soothing kind of thought that stimulates more and more thoughts and is actually relaxing versus challenging. Emotionally you are giving yourself a sun-shower of positive emotion throughout your system. You are literally tapping into the emotions that really nourish and relax you. Sometimes those emotions are sadness, like crying at a really good movie. Hard to believe crying can be relaxing, but it can. All the evidence is there to tell you that crying is cathartic, releasing harmful toxins and the body's way to let go of things it was unable to express. Being able to enjoy very deep emotional films is "Heart Play" for some people. You actually feel relaxed and at ease from the emotional experience. The theater and opera can evoke the same response. When I saw my first opera, *La Boheme*, at the age of fourteen, I cried my eyes out and had the best time of my life. I became a rabid opera fan, the sadder the better. We are by nature very emotive creatures. Our play can bring emotions to the surface and relaxation along the way.

Therapeutic

In talking about relaxation we can easily see the therapeutic feeling that play brings to our lives. I think kids have just got us kicked here when it comes to using the therapeutic effects of play to counter the stresses and strains of life. Think about it, after school kids go home and play. Now if you are one of those parents who insist the homework be done before the play starts I will be asking you to rethink your position at this time. Kids really understand the need to kick up their heels, unwind, decompress, whatever word works for you, to refresh and re-energize them.

Another good example of this is the much dreaded "car trip." Has every kid in America at one time or another been subjected to that road mania that hits Moms and Dads and leaves antsy little creatures buckled in the back? One of my interviewees mentioned that she lived in Europe for a great deal of her childhood. Her parents bundled them off every weekend to explore Europe, not wanting to miss taking advantage of their unusual opportunity to learn about many foreign countries. She and her brother absolutely hated every minute of it. They don't remember what they saw, but they do remember being cooped up in the car. After a week of school or work or working at home with the kids, people need the therapy that play brings.

Play rids us of the angst of the week and the problems of daily life. Play is like going to therapy but you don't have to pay for it! Now there could be the best reason ever to start playing!

10

Finding Your Unique "Heart Play," Nobody Else Gets To Have It!

Get out the shovels! We're going to find your "Heart Play" after years of hiding it under rocks!

One of the first things you get to do when you are finding your "Heart Play" is to rediscover how truly wonderful and unique you really are. I have this weird quirk that my good friends will testify to. I like to do things my own way. Interestingly enough they do, too. We are all very unique characters and we revel in the fun and different ways that we approach life. About the only thing we all agree upon is that we like to play and find as much joy in our lives as possible.

When you get up in the morning and put your feet on the floor you do it in your own unique way. Sure, I put my feet down too, but not like you. When you yawn and shake off the sleepiness of the night you are doing it your way. Check it out, watch your partner or your kids or someone on a sitcom. We each have our own way of doing things. This is good. This means that we also each have our own way of playing, too. That is part of what makes playing so much fun. It is a unique experience that changes your outlook on life and literally makes you be more you.

In order to get to your "Heart Play," it is necessary to explore this uniqueness further. In this fun exploration we will find out a little more about how you perceive yourself, your life, the work that you have chosen to do, the place you have chosen to live, the people you have chosen to have in your life, and finally the other things you do that express who you are.

First let us look at how you see yourself. Do you think that you are capable of playing and having a good time? You know, letting loose and doing what you really feel inside? Most people do not, so don't feel bad if you didn't have an instant yes to this question. We have been raised in a society of rules, laws, regulations and major league "shoulds." Remember the little kid who is noisy in the house will be told to "settle down." The child who is running and jumping will be told to "settle down." The kid who is so excited she is ready to burst at the seams to speak and keeps interrupting will be told to "settle down." Now after enough of this we begin to settle and settle and settle until we are in line and our enthusiasm is greatly curbed. Now I am not advocating that we raise children to be loud, out of control or rude. But I am saying that the next time a child does this in front of you that you might "settle them down" while not discouraging the excitement that they are feeling.

Now back to you as a "settled down" adult. You are fairly well indoctrinated that certain forms of play are totally acceptable and you can participate in these things if you behave in a lady-like manner. I will never forget the major flap over one of the women tennis players actually grunting when she served the ball. You would have thought that the world was coming to an end, such a faux pas! This was definitely not in the rules of tennis decorum. I love to watch people play tennis who do it for the pure joy of chasing the ball and celebrating each other's good shots. They laugh, they run, they hug when they are done. They may even grunt when they serve. They are PLAYING. Thus we go into our adult play and look at the structures, the rules, the dates, the scheduling, the planning, the training, regulating to death the things we love most. What is your unique way of playing? One of my friends absolutely refuses to keep score when she plays golf. She insists that it takes all the fun out of it for her. That's my girl! There was a great *Friends* episode on television where Rachel refuses to go jogging with Phoebe because Phoebe ran like a dweeb. Phoebe would throw her arms and legs out at strange angles and looked absolutely nuts as she ran along. Phoebe eventually convinces Rachel that running more like a child would be way more fun. The show ends with both of them running with arms and legs flailing out to the sides and the biggest smiles you have ever seen. They did not care about the stares they were engendering, they were playing.

My parents are avid pinochle players. They have their own way of playing this four-person game with two people. This serves them well when they travel or are home alone. They have found a way to be unique in their play. My mother also has puzzles and games at home for my sister and myself when we are there. She knows that we are never too old to play and that it is the secret to perpetual youth.

I used to love playing with papier mache. It felt really cool and gooey and you could make the most amazing things. As you can imagine mud pies and tadpoles were high on my list. From remembering these experiences I can see that I loved the touch and feel of water and water-based things. What can this tell me about what would be play for me now? Some days I actually do the dishes by hand just to get my water play. Go ahead you can laugh, but I make a great dinner guest because I'll do the dishes!

You must now take the time to go back in your life all the way to childhood. You should look at the way you played from your earliest memories right up to today. Write down in the left hand column of a piece of paper how you played between the ages of 5 and 7, then 8 and 11, then 12 to 14 and so on. You can use larger year increments when you hit your 20's, 30's and beyond. What did you used to do as a child or teen that was just plain fun and playful. Did you like to ride bikes? Did you climb trees? Swim in the river? What were all the playful things that you did? Spend a good deal of time looking this list over and enlarging it as memories come back to you.

I have been working on mine for two years and actually ask my sister, my mother, my childhood playmates (who I still gratefully have in my life). It is amazing the things that I have forgotten, yet they were so much fun for me. One recurring theme for me was water play. When we were little we swam every hot summer afternoon in the pond behind my house.

When I was a freshman in college I water skied almost every day before going to my summer job, waitressing at 4 o'clock. My sister, cousin and I rented a small sailboat and taught ourselves to sail. My Dad took us fishing in a rowboat. Before the pond was built we used to go down to the river. When I was in my twenties I organized a three day raft trip for twenty-one people. I had a summer house on the beach at Cape Cod so I could body surf and sleep on the beach (and nine roommates so we could afford it). My first year out of college I spent the entire summer trekking to the beaches north of Boston every weekend to play in the surf. All of this remembering led me to understand that I really like almost anything to do with the water, and therein lies some of my "Heart Play." To that end this summer I am learning to kayak. Okay, not the white water stuff, but gentle lake kayaking, which is in abundance where I now live.

Do you see how finding your "Heart Play" works? You have to go back and look at the unique you that you have been all your life, starting from first memory. You need to put these thoughts together and begin to see the pattern that is emerging from the things that were really playful and fun for you.

Now write opposite each of your great childhood memories what might be your comparable plan as an adult. Go wild! Write parachuting if you used to like high board diving. Write photography if you used to play with your parent's camera. Write sculpting if you made mud pies and snow castles. Write bicycling if you loved bicycling. There are no rules and there is no reality, just play with this one. Remember you are on a journey here to find your "Heart Play," just like looking for the right car, the right spouse, the right dress, you may have to weed through some stuff that's not quite right before you get to what is!

One of the biggest keys to finding your "Heart Play" is silence. Silence is a playful, wonderful time that makes no demands on us and requires us to do nothing but indulge in the thoughts that come our way. When you are working on your play history, try to find the quietest spot around you. Crawl into a closet, go to the top of a mountain, sit in the philosophy section of your local library, but find a quiet spot. Play itself is not always loud or noisy or busy. Sometimes play is to sit and think about the things you would like to do.

In finding our "Heart Play" one of the things you need to do is give yourself permission to daydream. Dream, in this silent space you have created, of things that would make your heart sing. **Do not edit the dream** because you do not have the time, the money, the skill, or whatever other reason you can conjure up for not doing what you are dreaming of.

Dream of being a child again and imagine the thrill of the playful things you used to do. This little exercise led me to the most fantastic experience I have had in a long time this past winter. One of the things I knew about my childhood was this fascination with being and playing outdoors. In the winter we sledded all the time. Often, my Dad couldn't make it up the hill from the main road to our house because we had been sledding all day and packed it down to solid ice (he wasn't very happy about that, by the way). This past winter I drove up to our cabin in the mountains, which has a very steep straight driveway, only to find about two feet of snow on it. Since I never drive up anything I wouldn't drive down, I left the car at the bottom and hauled my food and luggage up this thing. On one of the trips back down, I took the cooler back down with me to load up the odds and ends that were left in the car. For whatever reason I decided to sit on top of the cooler and rode it all the way to the bottom! I was sledding again. Excitedly I called home and told my husband, who was coming up the next day, to bring the kid's sleds! I then hooked up with a friend's children who were staying close by and spent hours the next day sliding down the driveway. To make it even better there were huge fluffy snowfields on either side of the driveway for the times we "crashed." I cannot remember the last time I had that much fun and we finished the afternoon with hot chocolate and popcorn. You know, play food.

Finding your "Heart Play" can actually take years. Once you embark on this journey you will have many fits and starts, chase a few dreams that really aren't play for you any more and nature may temper what you are now physically able to do. But don't give up. There are many, many things out there that you will find and eventually build into your life for greater joy, health and wealth.

One young woman I worked with was able to move to her "Heart Play" much faster than most. I thought you might enjoy how she got there so quickly and what some of the "aids" were that expedited the process. This woman agreed, after we began to talk, that she really did not have a clue what her "Heart Play" was. We went back and went over and over her childhood to no avail until we discovered something in the sixth grade. She had won her State award for Art in her age category. I was stunned. I knew this person and she was very talented in many ways, but I had never seen her indulge in anything artistic. She affirmed what I had observed and said she basically had not touched a pencil, paintbrush, charcoal or anything since that time. You met this woman earlier in the book when we discussed someone who did not take art classes as a teenager because of the peer pressure not to take a "dweeb" class. Over the next month I watched this woman begin to look for a way to express her art. One day she walked in and told me that she was going to a pottery shop that evening that allowed you to make your own pots and paint them. She was bringing a friend, some food and wine and planned to "paint her heart out." She will be playing with her art for the rest of her life. She has found her "Heart Play" and whenever life doesn't seem quite right she will be going to her play to get herself back on track. She is also someone who wants her career to eventually reflect her play, and she will be working on that for the next few years.

Finding your "Heart Play" is a magical experience. I was so dopey when I started this process that people around me just thought I had lost my mind. In a way I had. I had lost the mindset that I deserved to play, could have the time to play, the money, the skill, the talent or whatever else I needed, to play.

Do your homework and find your "Heart Play." It is well worth the effort and you will have the gifts of your labor for the rest of your life.

11
I'm Not An Athlete,
I'm An Athletic Supporter

In the women's stories collected for this book there emerged an interesting pattern for some of the women. Several women who had "high play" concepts for themselves demonstrated their play by watching others or playing at things that others were enjoying a lot more. Let me explain.

Quite often playing is actually watching someone else play. Car races, air shows, dance competitions, the circus, horse racing and so on. Another level of this may come from being a soccer Mom or a golf "widow." It is a belief that the fun for me is watching someone else play. Now with our kids, this can be very true. Sideline play can encompass all the joy of actual play, particularly if our team wins. Even with our spouse, this can be true as we cheer on a foursome or a team.

You have done it and enjoyed it. Concerts, theater, and sporting events all have the ability to bring enjoyment to you if they are things that you like. Where the danger comes in is when these are the only things you do for play, or they are more obligatory than fun. Here are some stories to explain what I mean.

Karen recounted to me a typical weekend schedule with her kids and fiancé, which she was expected to participate in. Starting with Friday night and wrapping up on Sunday night the schedule was full of dinners with friends, fitness workouts with one of the kids, an adventure trek, a gallery opening, a competitive race on Sunday morning, a family dinner on Sunday afternoon and whatever. Now Karen likes to do most of the things that are listed here. Time with her family and fiancé are important to her and enjoyable. However, there is apiece missing.

Karen's heart play is quiet, creative craftwork. She is extremely talented and can produce amazing things. Her heart sings when she spends time with her hands, creating. This requires quiet time, being alone to accomplish. There is one problem with the weekend schedule of her family; it has no room left in it for her to do her creative work. Karen is fairly far down the path of learning to have time for her "heart play" again, and she will now occasionally schedule time that is hers for creative work. It isn't as often as every week or weekend, but it is there and something she can use to bring joy into her life.

It is a dilemma to decide whether you should go along with what everyone else needs and wants you to do, or be selfish and give yourself the opportunity for "heart play." When we find our personal "heart play" we will forever have the option to practice it or not. When we have demands, such as children's events, we will go and enjoy them as much as possible. But if your child chooses to participate in everything from ballet to soccer with baseball, gymnastics and karate in between, you will have to decide what part you will play on the sidelines and when you will play for yourself.

Some moms have told me their time belongs to the kids and Mom's play is on hold until the kids do not need them so much. I cannot argue with this kind of support for our children. However, I wonder if we forget that our children are also using us as guides to how they might live as adults. Do we forget that we should model the behaviors of healthy adults so our children will know how to play when they grow up?

I asked all my interviewees to describe how their parents played and what they observed as children. I heard everything from my parents did not play at all, to my Mom and Dad were always doing something fun like dancing, bowling, fishing, playing cards and so on. One point of confusion was when the parents played with the children, such as board games and the like, versus adult play separate from the children. What is important in a child's life is that there is a little of both.

A young couple I know are constantly engaged with the kids from catch in the backyard to crafts in the kitchen. The house is full of play that is shared by all. The father is also one to play outside the house. He is a golfer and on a softball team. He may even be a bowler in the winter months. The mother's play is with the children and she is very content with this at the moment. She sees herself as an "athletic supporter" for this period of her life. Her mother's play was very similar. She was a "caregiver." She enjoyed taking care of the children, the house, her spouse and her parents. She did not "play" until her retirement recently when she became very involved with the local historical society. She is having a ball collecting, cataloguing and creating displays for her town. Delayed play is a wonderful gift, particularly when you have enjoyed your support role as much as these women have.

My parents both played outside the home, as well as attended all our sports and music events. An interesting thing about their play was the "scheduled" aspect of it. In other words Mom bowled on a set night each week or played cards on a set day on the weekend. Dad was on a similar schedule. To this day they have a calendar of events on their wall. But in their later years they have added much more extemporaneous play to their lives. What I missed the most as a kid was getting up on a Saturday and looking out at the sunshine and saying let's not work today but go to the lake or hike in the woods. One of the things I had to learn to play again was to realize that life is short, and that when the urge to play strikes you should take advantage of it. It is important to be open to play even when there is work to be done. It doesn't mean letting the lawn grow to three feet high or never getting the dishes done or the house cleaned, but letting yourself have the luxury of sometimes not doing those things on a schedule. Jean, who plays with her children all the time, holds the theory that spontaneity is critical to play. Remember the great Dr. Seuss book *The Cat In The Hat*? Its essence was about playing rather than working, yet the work got done in the end. I think Dr. Seuss knew what was in the heart of every kid and maybe every adult.

We have many people in our lives that need our time and attention and yes, we are taking care of them. They also have things that they want us to do with them. Your partner may have a very interesting and long agenda of great things to do, but you must look very carefully at this agenda and decide what works and what does not work for you. This issue is not one to be taken lightly. One of my dearest friends in the world told me that several years into her marriage she realized that her husband ALWAYS decided what they would do. He was not willing or able to allow for the "heart play" she was seeking. Although she had, and still has, great love for him they parted ways. She told me, " I lost myself when he always decided what we would do and eventually I went into complete despair." She did not want to live a life of despair, but of joy. The lack of "heart play" in our lives can have serious consequences.

We also have another interesting dilemma that comes up with our friends. The "let's go do.." syndrome. Let's go play golf, let's take a karate class, let's climb a mountain. The implication being that if you want to be with this person, you will go and do what they want to do. Now of course it is human nature to want to do things with our friends. Golf can be played alone, but a foursome of friends is a lot more fun. You can climb alone, but it is safer and more fun as a shared experience. Tennis alone just doesn't work for me. You can even ride a roller coaster alone, but if you scream and no friend hears, is it as much fun? It is important that we say yes to the things that are play for us and no to those that are not. A good friend is someone that you have some "thing" in common with, not necessarily everything. One of my best friends is an avid (make that AVID) golfer, I am not. Does that mean that we cannot play together? Absolutely not. We enjoy dinners, theater, books, lectures, creative work and much, much more.

I would like to give another perspective on playing "from the sidelines," so to speak. My Aunt Frances had a wonderful life full of fun. She always radiated a beautiful light and I used to run to her home every time I traveled to where she lived. Some people would probably not understand her as a "playful" person, as she lived in a totally "homebound" environment. She was not disabled, in fact she was extremely able bodied, but she found her play in her eight children, grandchildren, spouse, and house. When I interviewed her for this book she was a delight to listen to as she described all the play she had over the years of her life. She found play in her family's exploits, adventures and rich conversations on many topics. Her home was filled with life, love and exploration, even if much of that exploration was done by others. Her flowers and garden were indicative of the nature she nurtured in those children and the joy of play they had together. She is also the only person I know who had never missed a day of "The Guiding Light," one of her quirkier play things. Frances had a laugh that showed play was in her life. Maybe it looked like work to us, but she was having fun. Maybe it was quiet and out of the "norm" for the world, but it was play for her. I am blessed to have had this role model of what a playful "athletic supporter" can look like. She taught me that play is sometimes very, very quiet and very, very powerful in its simplicity.

There is a great book that came out years ago called *Soar With Your Strengths*, by Donald Clifton and Paula Nelson. They tell a great story about a woman trying to do what others do and be good at it or like it. For over seven years this woman tried to master skiing. She was absolutely terrified of the sport and even took Librium to cope with her fears of lifts, slopes and the sport in general. She was also not good at it. What she was really good at was tennis. The book goes on to tell us that she was addicted to mastering a weakness because she was fueled by others' stories in the lodge of a "great run." So she was looking for her great run. We need to be cautious about how much we are influenced by the fun someone else is having, and thinking that this should also be fun for us. I have kept Clifton and Nelson's book on a shelf close to me all my life because I am easily persuaded this way. My biggest failure in this area was golf. I took up this sport years ago along with many of my friends. I bought the clubs, took countless lessons and even played in a league at one point. Now you will need to use your imagination here to understand how bad I was at this game, but think of swinging and missing all the time, sand traps, balls in the bottom of lakes or across the road from the course and so on. This was and is not my game. I love to watch it on TV. I can even enjoy hearing people talk about it. I do not enjoy playing it. But all my friends were playing and I wanted to go along too. One day, after I left a club on the ninth hole in the grass, missed the sixth hole completely because my partner and I could not find it, and whiffed at the ball on the tee enough times to make a breeze over the course, I woke up. My awakening included allowing my friends to play without me and allowing myself to go and find other forms of play that would make my heart sing versus giving me a heart attack.

Our decision to be athletic supporters or athletes is ours. Our decision to attend or participate in events that are play for others, but not for us, is ours. Listen carefully to your heart and decide wisely.

12
Making Play
A Part of Your Life—
How Hard Can That Be?

In order for this book or anything else on play to have any impact on your life, you must begin to make play a part of your life in every way possible. It is actually possible that almost everything in life could be fun or playful. But you must make playing and thinking of life in a more lighthearted manner a part of you. This allows real "Heart Play" to reveal itself to you. In addition, even after you find your initial "Heart Play," you are going to find that you are growing and evolving in the world. There will be new opportunities for you to play and work in environments and situations that are not known to you at this time. For example, what if you were suddenly asked to move to a new city, state or country? Not going to happen? You don't know that. Don't want to do it? Maybe not today, but someday there could be a very compelling reason for you to change your mind.

This new openness to play and to have playful thinking can make your life much more enjoyable and livable. That's right—livable. So often we "live" in things that we do not care for very much. Let's take one of my favorites, commuting. I used to think that there was absolutely nothing livable about commuting. Then I decided to apply my playful thinking to this requirement in my life. First, there is always the radio. Morning talk show hosts are very entertaining to some folks. They can start your day with a good laugh, get you thinking about some pretty zany stuff or just have you distracted. Then there are the OTHER DRIVERS. You know these people, the ones that can ruin a beautiful day by tailgating, cutting you off, braking suddenly or a thousand other little irritants. Here is where your playful thinking should get its morning workout. First, the person who is tailgating you is doing it because they, number one, need to get somewhere really quickly and are checking out your car to see if it can be used as a ramp to fly over the bumper-to-bumper traffic. Number two, they are from the FBI, CIA, or IRS and you look very much like someone they are chasing down and are trying to get a better look to decide whether to capture you or not. Or number three, they are actually tied to the bumper of your car with a rope and are using you to conserve fuel. Do you see how it goes? By the time I get to my destination in the morning I have usually had three or four really good adventures with my fellow commuters. The one they love the most is the BIG SMILE at the red light. At first there is usually the natural smile back, but then there are a few furtive looks that reflect the consternation at receiving a free smile. Why me? Did I do something? Are they flirting with me? Do I know them? Picture in your mind for a moment what it would be like to drive in Manhattan if every driver were required to smile at every other driver at each red light! Hand gestures replaced by smiles.

Now on to the office. Once again, you are challenged to look at the first person you see when you come in the door and smile. Don't feel like it? Do it anyway. It is really more for you than for them. This will allow you to understand more about what you like and do not like about your work. It will help you do your work better and with a sense of joy. I recently had some major surgery and was in the hospital for pre-op, then the operating room, then recovery, then to a regular room until I could be stabilized to go home. Let me give you this experience from the play perspective. When I checked in at the desk I was told to "take a seat and someone will be with you soon." No smile. My nervousness increased slightly, but I was still okay. Then I was greeted by a nurse who took me into pre-op and began the story of what was going to be happening. She looked me in the eye, she smiled, she cracked some jokes and generally I was totally ready by the time she was done, both physically and mentally. My doctors stopped by and smiled and told me the things they were planning to do. We discussed whether they had gotten a good night's sleep or had been out partying all night and other amusing stories to put me at ease. When I awoke I was in terrible pain, but a smiling face with a kind voice told me I was receiving all the medication I could safely receive for pain and that I would be feeling better soon. I still was hurting terribly physically, but somehow I was better overall. In my room over the next few days I alternately had smiling, funny people or flat-faced, serious people. You'll never guess which ones gave me more comfort.

Now I know we are all not healing professionals in the technical sense of the word. But, we are in the process of healing ourselves about play. It is going to take the same dedication to look at the world with joy to find our "Heart Play" and to DO our "Heart Play." We will have to look at when we smile and when we are flat-faced. I do not smile all the time; you may not smile all the time. Eventually you will smile more, you will get more smiles and you will open yourself up to what is joyful for you and what is not.

I mentioned my commuting earlier. I have learned over time that I am good in a commute up to 35 minutes. If it is longer than that no amount of "playfulness" will penetrate my boredom of driving. I now know that the work I do and where I live must match this truth about me. I also know that I get hungry, thirsty and sometimes antsy in the car. I have water, food and lots of tapes and CDs of all different types to keep me distracted and stimulated. Now I even have a traveling companion, Dolly. She is a large stuffed doll with a big red nose and even bigger smile. One look at her and I crack up. So do the people who pull up along side me and see her sitting in her seatbelt in my passenger seat. The people I am going to meet or see at my destination should not be the victims of my long and boring commute. They are innocent victims and potentially keys to my future play, so I want them happy and responsive to me.

What happens when you are playful and smiling and no one is smiling back? Some would say welcome to the real world. I say, "Bring them on!" Inside every one of them is someone who is playful, ready to come out. They may not want to come out and play today, but someday. One day in my search for luncheon protein, I pulled into Arby's. Despite the lunch hour, almost no one was there. The clerk who waited on me never saw me. She kept her eyes down, her voice talked to the floor and after she took my order and my money she then disappeared to talk to a friend. Okay, not her day to play. I accept that. When I moved down the counter to wait for my order I caught the eye of the guy who slices the meat and makes the sandwiches. I gave him the biggest smile my face could produce. You know what? He gave me back an even bigger smile. We smiled at each other the whole time he was making my sandwich and I felt great and I am betting so did he. He probably took that smile to someone else and I hope they gave him one too. Do we have the solution to world peace here?

When I am teaching people to find their "Heart Play," this exercise of putting play into your everyday life is a critical part of the course. You need to feel good when you get out of bed in the morning and look forward to the day. This is true even if it involves going to the dentist, dealing with a really ugly work problem, meeting with a school counselor because your kid is in trouble, going to court for a speeding ticket and then cooking dinner for six people you don't like. You can still feel good about your day. Get in the shower and sing. Can't sing, take a radio in there and lip sync and dance. Step out of the shower with joy. Know that you will do your best that day and your only job is to find some joy in the situation by playing with it. Before you sit in the dentist chair ask him what his or her favorite movie or food or dog is, and why. They will immediately think of something they like, which puts them in a good mood and then they will be feeling good while working on you. That's what I want from my dentist while she's crawling around me with a drill.

The work problem? They exist. They happen. What can you put into the situation playfully, but respectfully, that will help ease the tension and get to a good solution? Sometimes, with something as simple as having no chairs for the meeting, words are often said differently with everyone standing up. Maybe starting the meetings by asking everyone what good things have happened to him or her recently. Set the tone, create the scene. One thing I tried once was to put a silly red nose on everyone while they discussed a serious financial crisis for the organization. Did it work? You bet. When the group donned the noses they began to speak from their heart and their hearts said they knew they could create some savings to avoid layoffs. The company passed through the crisis successfully and no one was laid off.

There was a company in Malvern, Pennsylvania that had the most incredible meeting rooms. They were full of toys and hats and gizmos to keep people thinking. They also had a flag system outside the door to let the rest of the company in on the progress they were making. The green flag meant things were going well and people would walk by smile and wave and encourage the workers in the room. The yellow flag said things were not going so well and we could use your thoughts, if you are not busy on something else. The red flag said we are in real trouble here and need everyone from the janitor to the president in the room to help us solve the problem. When that happened there were people sitting on the floor, standing, hanging from the rafters, but everyone was giving whatever crazy idea they have to the group. This company never missed a deadline with this program in place.

Next we are going to school to meet the counselor. Probably not the best place for playfulness. That is unfortunate. Our schools have become regulated and processed to a point that it makes solving the problems a lot harder than it should be. There is a great story in the book *Imagery For Getting Well*, by Deirdre Davis Brigham that explains what playfulness and discipline can look like. Deirdre's father was an educator that ran an all boys school. Once a situation arose where a group of boys were showing off by a lake in front of the school. Several fell in and became drenched. When the bedraggled children presented themselves to her father and begged for dry clothes he responded, "You have broken the rules, and you have a choice. Either you can take off all your wet clothes and go around with nothing on, or you can use a couple of these Santa suits which are nice and dry to finish out the day." I love this story. What is the "Santa suit" to your child's problem? I am not talking about humiliating them, but finding out how to touch their playful side to get the point across. Maybe they should be required to write something humorous, or design a shadow box, or build a birdhouse to represent the jailhouse they don't want to go to. We are always punishing to get our point across, rather than creating awareness. What if after you got too many points on your license, instead of losing it you were required to teach driver's education in a parking lot or classroom? When we teach, we learn.

Our next stop for the day is court. You "bumped" a guy at a red light and got a ticket. I would not play with the District Attorney or the Judge! However, you are probably there because you made a mistake. We all do. They happen all the time. You are a good person though and the best way to get through this is to think about the gift you will give yourself when this is over. Maybe a special dinner, a trip, a small item from the store. Maybe just some quiet time in a hot bath to think about all the good things you do that cancel out this one little mistake. Your time in court should be focused on the good thing you are going to do for yourself and the good person you are. This is a way of playing with the tough stuff, by having a counterpoint to it.

Well, it's time for that dinner party. Six people, all business colleagues of your partner, or people from your homeowners association or the school soccer committee. Not exactly stimulating conversationalists for you. Or are they? Everyone on this planet has the gift of play in him or her, even if they don't show it, acknowledge it or speak about it. How do I know this? Because they were kids once. They have played before. Need a conversation lead? Ask them what they liked to play the most as a child. Watch the conversation take off, as they wistfully describe everything from special places to what they made with mud. You will be amazed.

Tired? End your days playfully with cartoons before you go to bed. They are now on television twenty-four hours a day or as near as your local paper.

Live your life with play as a criteria for your days. Rent a humorous video every other week and just laugh and love it. Maybe it is even something you have seen before. I rent Julia Roberts movies because her funny faces and antics always make me laugh. Buy a collection of *Calvin and Hobbes*. They are wonderfully philosophical and humorous at the same time. Calvin is always looking for a new way to play. There is a website called Good Clean Funny Jokes that will send a humorous story to you every day on your email. No ads, no spamming, just fun. Too busy to read them, delete the ones you don't have time for. No one will come looking for you if you don't read it.

Watch for play every day. It is all around you. Rollerbladers in the park, improvisation at the local comedy club, children in the play area at the mall—life is full of play, we just aren't looking hard enough if we aren't seeing it.

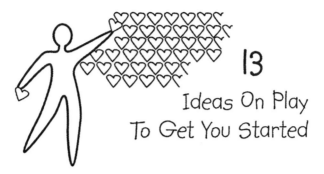

13
Ideas On Play
To Get You Started

It is time to look at the many different ways you might play. In this chapter there are many lists. These lists are for the purpose of stimulating thoughts about things you might enjoy doing for playful activities. The best way to read this chapter is to pay close attention to the things you might have done in the past and the FEELINGS that they evoke when you think about them now.

Another thing to look for are the many things you may never have done, still might not try, but that nonetheless grab your attention. Let me give you an example. You might have looked at kayaking as fun on the water, but you also might have seen enough videos of those white water daredevils to know that you are not going to risk life and limb tucked inside a little plastic boat in a raging river. If you stayed with that feeling of being out on the water and even the kayak, you might conjure up another way to kayak, that is with a wide mouthed version of a kayak on a very gentle lake. This is achievable by almost everyone.

With this in mind do not score things as out of the question too quickly. If there is something about the item that is listed that speaks to you, give it a "maybe" score until you can check it out some more and rule it out completely. Really go for your "gut feeling" when reading these lists. Let your intuition guide you along to check "maybe" next to things that catch your eye, even though you are pretty sure you will never do them.

In using this process, you are creating a list for exploration of new play-things that could last a lifetime. I encourage you to write in other ideas that you have seen or heard about at the end of the list you will compile.

Here is what we are going to do at this point. We are going to read through this list and give every item a score according to the following scale.

Never in a million years—Score it "3"

Maybe, would need to convince myself, or explore it more—Score it "2"

Absolutely, I either have done or currently do this and love it or I have always wanted to try this—Score it "1"

The best way to do this scoring is to take your initial reactions in a quiet place. Then go back and rethink all 2's and 3's. Quite often people find that they put down a 3 only to say, "well maybe," which means it is a 2. Often a 2 can turn into 1, because you really have a desire to try this, even if it is for one time. Raft trips, sky diving, and mountain climbing quite often fall into this category.

The lists here have been categorized by things like music, outdoor/adventure, outdoors, competitive sports, solo sports, social based, home based, crafts to share, etc.. The reason for this is that while we could never put every conceivable way to play into lists, we can get you to learn more about yourself in the types of things that catch your attention.

Look at items that we have been general on, such as collecting, and see if there is something you are collecting without even knowing about it. This might be something that you could get into more once you acknowl-edge that what you have been doing it, subtly, almost unconsciously, and it may have some of your "Heart Play" in it.

I discovered this when I mentioned to my husband that I was the activity junkie and he was the collector in our family. He responded, "what about the animals?" What I had not realized was that I had been collecting various statues of animals in glass, woodcarving and metal sculpture. Looking further, I found I was really into collecting fish. I had all types of fish, in glass, wood and ceramics, all in different rooms for different accents. When I put them together I had quite the collection! Now I enjoy going to new places with this knowledge that I am a small collector and looking for new "fish" for my home.

To the lists! Read these slowly, and remember that you may need to look twice at some things. Certain activities that fall into different categories appear more than once. Have fun; put maybes next to anything that you pause at. Remember we won't come and look for you to make you do them!

Competitive Sports

Volleyball
Soccer
Softball
Baseball
Football
Basketball
Horseshoes
Golf
Foosball
Pool
Car Racing
Ice Hockey
Rugby
Field Hockey
Triathlons
Racquetball
Tennis
Marathons
Darts
Air Hockey

Solo Sports

Golf
Walking
Running
Bicycling
Skiing
Snow Shoeing
Snowboarding
Snorkeling
Scuba Diving
Water skiing
Windsurfing
Parasailing
Jet Skiing
Horseback Riding, Jumping
Motorcycling
Hiking
Swimming
Kayaking
Sailing
Fishing
Surfing
Ice Skating
Roller Blading
Roller Skating
Rock Climbing
Other_____

Sports with Friends

White Water Rafting
Items from above lists _____
Other

Sports
Watching Major League, Minor League or College Games
Baseball
Football
Basketball
Hockey
Gymnastics
Golf
Car Racing
Wrestling
Horse Racing
Soccer
Rugby
Dog Racing
Ice Skating
Dance Competitions
Tennis
Other_____

Little League
Observing
Coaching
Booster
Other_____

Exercise as Play for You
Jazzercise
Pilates
Kickboxing
Karate
Tai Chi
Boxing
Stair Stepping
Aerobics

Treadmill
Weightlifting
Cycle Karaoke
Pole Dancing
Yoga
Dahn Hak
Other_____

Outdoor/Adventure

Mountain Climbing
White Water Rafting
Rock Climbing
Other_____

Outdoors

Gardening
Landscaping

Games

Computer Games
PlayStation/Nintendo
Crossword Puzzles
Board Games
Card Games
Charades
Pictionary
Gambling
Jigsaw Puzzles

Collecting

Books
Antiques
Art
Cars
Plates
Thimbles

Spoons
Music
Movies
Statuary
Comic Books
Postcards
Dolls
Cookbooks
Collectibles
Other _____

Cooking

Dinner Parties
Experiments for Family
Contests
Specialties (e.g. sauces, desserts, main dishes)
Home Brewing
As gifts for others or bake sales

Music

Playing an instrument
Singing
Dancing
Attending Musical Events
Listening
Collecting
Bell Ringing
Dancing
Other_____

Crafts/Hobbies

Sewing
Quilting
Knitting
Crochet or Cross-stitch

Making Ginger Bread Houses
Origami
Beading
Tapestry
Furniture Refinishing
Flower Arranging
Painting
Drawing
Pottery
Sculpting
Toile Painting
Macramé
Graphic Design
Wall Painting
Photography
Cooking
Baking
Dinner Parties
Wine Tasting
Flower Gardening
Vegetable Gardening
Lawn Care
Landscaping
Home Decorating
Fashion Design
Interior Design
Remodeling
Watching TV
Watching Movies (Old or New)
Reading
Writing
Meditating

Amateur and Ham Radio
Telescopes
Aquariums
Astronomy
Beach Combing
Birding
Books
Bubbles
Candle Making
Cloud Watching
Clowning
Electronics
Fire Eating
Flying Planes (remote or real)
Genealogy
Glass Blowing
Hand Writing Analysis
Hang Gliding
Hot Air Ballooning
Jet Engines
Juggling
Kites
Knotting
Lock Picking
Magic
Metal Work
Models
Pottery
Puppetry
Pyrotechnics
Racing Cars (remote or real)
Railroad, Trains

Rockets
Rocks, Gems, Minerals
Sailing Boats (remote or real)
Scrapbooks
Soap Making
Stained Glass
String Figures
Textiles
Treasure Hunting
Urban Exploration
Museums
Winemaking
Other_____

Dancing

Belly Dancing
Ballroom
Rock and Roll
Line Dancing
Country Western
Polka
Salsa
Jazz
Other_____

Theater/Cultural Events

Acting
Props
Staging
Directing
Writing Plays
Fund Raising
Opera
Symphony

Ballet
Theater
Musicals
Other_____

Solitude

Meditation
Sitting In Silence
Sitting In Silent Observation
Praying

Animals

Breeding
Showing
Walking Your Dog
Training
Playing With Your Animal
Watching

Educational

Taking Courses
Surfing the Web
Studying On Your Own
Learning New Skills
Other_____

Miscellaneous

Shopping
Lunch/Dinner With Friends
Participating in Charity Events
Romantic Dinner with Significant Other
Playing With Your Kids
Volunteering
Travel
Adventure

Amusement Parks
Theme Parks
Political Causes
Other_____

Now that we have read a rather exhaustive list, you need to take a few moments and see what themes about your play have developed. Did you find yourself replaying some old tapes about what used to be fun, like flag football in the Fall? Did you find yourself in more of an observer role in your play?

This list is by no means complete. We are wonderful in our unique ways to have fun that others would never think of as playful. Maybe you climb a tree when the urge strikes, or stand on your head. Play is a mysterious and exciting adventure for the heart. I believe you will find yourself looking more carefully at many of the things you do and enjoy, and finding that there is more play in your life than you knew.

With this list in mind, challenge yourself to not only try what you loved and may have given up, but also to try new things. Often one thing leads to another and what is really playful for us may be "behind the scenes." As an example, I once knew a man, Howard, who thought that being the referee in a yacht race was playful. He didn't want or need to be a racer. He loved being part of the event, sitting in his boat and marking the boats as they made their turns in the course. As I have said before, finding your "Heart Play" is like every journey in that we make some wrong turns, some long turns, and have to travel through some not-so-great things to get to better things.

Now recheck your marks as I mentioned earlier and see what new things might be in store for you in the coming year. If something tickles your fancy, even if it is outrageous, begin to research it on the web. Talk to friends, find people who have some experience in the area and gather data.

One of the most critical parts of getting our "Heart Play" back in our lives is to get the information we need, whether it is the price of supplies and equipment, or learning the necessary skill. Life offers fascinating opportunities in many ways to get us into our play. Often you can find free lessons or sample classes. I have a good friend who offers a painting class for people who just want to "throw" paint on a canvas. No hassle, no critique, just painting fun. You can find these things with a little homework, and amazingly enough this homework is really play, as it gets you on your way.

I got a good demonstration of the way play "stretches" out over time through a story from one of my students. She told me that her play was travel. Knowing that her job allowed little time for such play I asked why she felt it was play all year long. She quickly explained that her annual trip was an extended one involving months of research and planning to maximize everything about the exotic place. This really shows how play homework is also definitely play.

14   Valuing Women's Play

It would be hard to write a book like this without exploring the topic of valuing women's play. In a world where the major television stations devote weekend afternoons to sports and the next biggest channels, after the networks, are ESPN and Fox Sports, it isn't hard to understand what I am trying to point to. Now one of the first things you will hear is that weekday afternoons are devoted to soap operas and talk shows for women. While that is true, the viewing audiences are significantly less. But, let's not quibble about television, because we have already decided that isn't play most of the time.

It is an interesting study to talk to women about their definition of play and then their practice of the same. When we begin this journey to find our "Heart Play" it is typical that people will look to what is the "norm" for play to see if it is something they should be doing. In this book I list lots of things you might do for play. We have everything from the more acknowledged forms of play to some obscure thoughts and ideas.

This gives you a great menu to stimulate thinking about what might be play for you. You may choose something that seems of little value to the world overall, particularly others who are an important part of your life. If you or your loved ones approach the "Heart Play" activity with that in mind, trouble may be in the making. We talked earlier about someone leaving her job because her boss would not allow her to play at work. Now what about a boss who does not approve of your play that may require you to leave early some days, or take a long weekend now and then? What about a spouse who believes that what you are doing is "silly" or frivolous and is not supportive of helping with the kids or house so that you will have time to do your play? What about friends or children that react in a similar way?

I see real examples of this among women all the time. Someone will be trying to organize a get-together of some kind. They will ask someone to skip their play to be at the get-together, basically sending the message that "Heart Play" is at the bottom of the list of things we should do.

Women's play most likely does not have a "World Series," a "Stanley Cup," an " Oscar," or even a championship. By not having these competitive elements to it there can be a sense of less value. I have a good friend who raises bees and makes honey. She loves being with her bees, being outdoors and bottling the honey for her own use as well as for gifts. She has found real "Heart Play." This is a solitary pursuit, one with a simple outcome. We are all the beneficiaries of her honey, (which by the way is great), but does her play receive the same value from her family and friends as her husband's softball? Now my friend really doesn't care if it does or doesn't. It really doesn't matter if it does or not, except when life intrudes and you don't get to your play. Softball games are scheduled, you know when and where they will be every week. The bees have a slightly more flexible schedule, so household chores and other obligations could potentially draw time away from them.

So often men's play is bigger, grander and more socially honored. Women are embarrassed to say that they would like to just "sit and knit." That is why we are talking about valuing women's play. Quite frequently women will not pursue their "Heart Play" because they lack the support that comes so naturally to men's play. It is not that you necessarily need other's support, or even care if they know what you do to play. What does matter is that you have the time and the space and the things you need to play as your heart dictates.

I have to tell you about some of the feedback and comments that I received from women when I began to work on this book and my seminars. It seems there are many women who feel they play just fine, and do not appreciate or understand that there are others who do not. In the course of talking to these women who claimed to already know how to play well, I found an interesting contradiction in our conversations. Someone would be telling me about his or her play, but they could not tell me what it did for them. In other words, they would tell me they went hiking that weekend and covered twenty miles a day. When I asked what they got out of it they would tell me that it was great exercise. Now I just finished a five-mile hike a few minutes before writing this and it was also good exercise, but there was more. At one point we just sat down on the ground and soaked up the vistas around where we were. We noticed that the soil suddenly changed from beige to a bright red under our feet. We found a grove of aspen trees that were speckled like cows and took pictures to enjoy later. My point here is that so often play is looked at as a quantity commodity versus a quality experience. People value twenty miles more than five with red dirt and "cow trees." Many women are playing now to meet the quota of time-off for play rather than finding their true "Heart Play."

Women often find so much pleasure in so many more "simple" pursuits. (I have quotationed simple, because nothing about knitting was ever simple for me). Women may have play that does not have crowds standing on their feet to watch them "win" or academies giving awards. They often have very, very quiet play. Because it is quiet it may not receive the value it deserves. While I have spoken of the value perceived by others, the real issue here is the value we perceive.

In my story I told you about my "silence" play. It is remarkable to me how long I believed that sitting still and doing nothing was not a good thing to do. I think we all get mixed up over some of the simple stuff we do every day and don't give it the value it deserves as being part of our play. My beekeeper friend is also a fabulous cook. She is playful with her time in the kitchen and cooking is part of her "Heart Play." Many women in my explorations "loved to cook," but they didn't see it as play because it was expected of them so it became just work and of little value.

Women often have "Heart Play" that does not seem like play, thus causing both the women and those around them to denigrate the value of the effort and the time spent on the activity. One form of women's play that truly needs to receive its proper value is communication. Women enjoy getting together to talk. Notice I did not say gossip, but talk. Women are very evolved in sharing their thoughts, feelings, ideas, skills and emotions. A group with much in common can have a very playful time talking, listening, encouraging, and sharing. This is absolutely one of my favorite forms of play. Lunch with a friend is so "heart" inspiring for me, that I often work ten times harder after such a session and enjoy every moment of my work. I talk, I listen, and I always LEARN, which is why this form of play is so much fun for me.

Today I listened to a story about my sister's husband coming home after a movie on a warm Saturday evening. When they got to the house he looked at her and said, I need to go out for just a little while. His "Heart Play" is his motorcycle. He gets to ride it to work every day, therefore playing to and from his way to work. He also just plays on it any time the mood strikes him. His evening ride through the canyons outside Denver made his heart sing. He values that play, as do many others.

Learn to think of whatever you choose for play as valuable. Do not let anyone's words or actions discourage you when you find what makes your heart sing. If you find how you are spending your play time valuable to you, then that is all that matters.

15

Time Wasters and Miracle Cures

A common theme when we talk about play is time or the lack of time. Life is very busy and there are many demands on everyone. I have always chuckled over those classes on balance that told me I needed to be sure that I had work, family, exercise, nutrition, spirituality, community service, financial security, rest, play, household chores, etc. all balanced out. I was usually exhausted when they finished the list and not interested in doing any of them. Oh yes, I forgot, also have a love life.

So when are we going to find time to play? I have two answers to that. The first goes like this, if you needed a new heart and I told you that you had to go get it on Tuesday or die, would you go on Tuesday or would you be too busy? The second is that play is in all the things that are listed above.

Let's start with the first. You are busy, your are going, doing, working, trying to rest, trying to stay in shape, trying to be a good mother, wife, employee, daughter, mate, sister and friend. My question to you is, are you trying to live your life in a manner that brings joy to you? Not just live and be okay, but live and be full of joy. If you are not seeking true joy in your life, then you will never be all those good things you are trying to be for other people. You are withholding the joy that is in you from them.

Nicolle is a woman who lives without great wealth. She works very hard to support three children all by herself. Her days are long, her burden great, but she still finds time to play. Not as much as she would like, but the children are growing and time will be more and more available to her and to her play. Her house is not perfect. The laundry is done, but not always put away. The dishes get done, in time. She is a joy to her children, her sister, her mother and her friends. More than that, she is able to cope with her burdens because she is joyful. Whenever I see this woman she always cheers me up and makes me feel so good about life. She never complains about not having enough time to play! She just makes play out of everything that comes her way, from dinner to homework with the kids, to visiting with me!

We have a huge list of things we need to get done. My friend, Jack, takes most of his vacations to complete what he refers to as the "honey do" list. I know this gentleman's income and suggested that he is perfectly capable of hiring someone to paint his house, but he said his wife wanted him to do it because he would do a better job. Now therein lies the crux of our too much to do and no time to play. Most things that need to get done are because of our expectation of perfection, or timeliness or because it is the "responsible" thing to do. My seminars inevitably come around to many of the household chores that take time and I inevitably shoot holes at the theory that these things must get done the way our mothers and grandmothers did them. Here is one that is always funny. Making the bed. Now I personally like to get into a made bed, you know smooth sheets, blankets all lined up, etc. I do not like to make beds so I use a comforter so it is easy to pull up the sheets and blankets and the put the comforter over the top. Not perfection but quick. I asked one class participant who hated bed making to tell me whom she made it for. She told me that no one comes into her house while she is at work during the day and creeps in her bedroom, so I ask again, who is the bed being made for? Now I am not advocating that we all suddenly become sloppy housekeepers, ignore the dishes, leave the beds unmade and don't take out the garbage. But I am suggesting that you figure out what you are doing and why and then find a way to make it fun or quit it! When my friend Mary was first married she did not have a dishwasher or much time, and she loved and still loves to play. Her solution was the oven. She loaded her dirty dishes in there for several days, and then hauled them out when she had time to wash or ran out! At the time I thought she was nuts, but in hindsight I know she was just trying to figure out what was important and do it in the order that let her be happy.

One of our seminar people had a problem with folding laundry. She could wash and dry it but it wasn't making it to the drawers. Now this is hard to ignore, particularly if it is all over the house. The group came up with a solution called "folding movie night." She now picks up a video one night a week on the way home and watches it while she folds the laundry. Remember what I said, figure out why you are doing it, get it out of the way, and then make it fun or stop.

My friend Brenda just stopped. It makes other people nuts, but it works for her family. She pulls all the laundry out and hangs up the shirts and pants and piles the rest on the laundry room counter. Everyone knows where to go to get clean underwear. The time she would spend folding and distributing laundry she spends doing arts and crafts with her children, which by the way is also her "Heart Play." She loves arts and crafts and until adopting this method of living she never had time to "play" at them. When guests come, the laundry room door is closed.

We could go on and on with methods and thoughts on how to move these household chores into the "play" category or circumvent them, but they are not our only time wasters. Our jobs, for which we get paid, can do the same thing. I just love the complaint of no time to play from those who think nothing of working until eight o'clock at night. Or the people who can tell me all the story lines from the sitcoms or drama shows from the night before. We are in a world that demands a lot of us in our jobs and I understand that there are times when we need to put in a few extra hours. But the person who does it day after day, week after week is either having a heck of a lot of fun and forgot to tell us that, or is so insecure about their skills that they feel the only way to assure their employment is to work harder.

Having come from a career in Human Resources I must tell you that long hours are not necessarily viewed by all managers as being the smartest way to get things done. First of all, the person who is always willing to stay late and do the extra work is considered a patsy. You heard me, a patsy, or someone to take advantage of because they are not smart enough to say no. Well you say they are the ones who get the promotions and the big bucks. Really? Sometimes that is true, but I have seen many people who work fairly regular hours and do good work who also get promotions and big bucks. If your company bases it's promotions and raises not on what you do but how long you stay, you may want to think again about where and what you are doing. Many professions have set hours and then ask for overtime when they get behind. If you can use the extra money it does not hurt to do this occasionally. If you are doing it all the time, you have to reconcile your desire to buy things with your desire to have joy and play in your life. The things you are buying may fill some temporary need you may have, but sometimes there are cheaper substitutes that do just as well.

Let me give you an example. I like nice things, but as with most I have champagne tastes to go with by beer pocketbook. Last year when I needed a new comforter and sheets for my bed I went to Target and bought a complete set for a little under one hundred dollars. At some of the "better" stores there was a similar set for three times the price I paid. Now there are some minor quality differences, but nothing noticeable to the naked eye or rough on the skin. I have received numerous comments on the beautiful set and I accept them all with a giggle. To work all those extra hours to get something that is barely different just does not make sense to me.

Now if the extra work is for medical bills, or debt from some previous problem there is obviously a difference. But in today's world there are so many ways to seek aid, consolidate debt, get refinancing and so on that they should be explored before you work yourself to death.

We need to find miracle cures to the things that take us away from our time to play. Part of the reason for my play journey was because I could not find the time to play. It is so ingrained in me to work, be responsible and be there for others that I would think it frivolous and wasteful to really take any significant time to play. I was so bad that I once flew over 2500 miles to a beautiful vacation location and took work with me! Now I am hoping that you are not that far gone, but if you are not taking the time each day, each week, each month to play and have fun for yourself you are close to my level.

I talked earlier about making your commute fun. I travel with "Dot" these days. She is a large stuffed re-creation of an old animated cartoon character. She sits in my passenger seat and smiles all the way to work and back. Nothing gets her down. She is my miracle cure to a real time waster for me, commuting.

There are so many times in our lives that we can find another thing to be done and give that priority over taking the time for a walk, a swim, playing an instrument or singing a quick song. Maybe we need to take a moment to sit quietly and listen to the wind or feel the sun on our face. Miracle cures work in this way. When one of those times comes up for you in the future, when you just work, work, work just stop and play instead. You can try it once for just a few minutes. Start simply. Close your office door and dance like crazy for five minutes then continue in your work. You have just had your first "Play Miracle."

Now you need to look at your week, and set aside some time to research your play life. Where will it happen for you this week? Lunch with a friend is a simple, quick way to get started. Maybe a long phone call to an old friend you haven't seen or spoken to in a while. Schedule it in and keep that appointment!

I always challenge people to look at how "WARPED" they are when they set about planning their lives. "WARPED" is my acronym for the following things we should have on our calendars:

W = Work

A = Administrivia (My word for the chores of life)

R = Rest

P = Play

E = Exercise

D = Devotional

When you do a "WARPED" inventory you look at each of these items, set some priorities then check those priorities against what is happening to you every day.

As an example last night I got eight hours of sleep, I will work eight hours today, I have planned a one hour hike that will be both playful and exercise for me. I will do the dishes, make the bed, write some thank you notes, check in with the kids, and do some light cleaning for a while. I have started and will end my day with some devotional exercises. I will not waste time in front of the TV. I probably will sneak in a game of Yatzee with my husband and I will sing while I wash the dishes, and maybe stop by the piano, on the way through that room, for one quick song. I am, and want to be, totally "WARPED!"

Since family is a critical and integral part of our lives I automatically include them in the "WARPED" activities. This means that I work with my family, we play together, and we do chores together and we can also do devotional things together and exercise together. For all these reasons, they do not get a separate category, as some people tend to do. Family is part of us through and through and we cannot only be playful for ourselves, but with others.

If you have young children and work full-time you will have to look at how you can use these guides to give you the time you need with them and for yourself. You may need to "miracle cure" some chores by making them playful. Singing and dancing while you do the dishes is permissible. Making a game out of picking up toys is easy and kids get the right idea about the "administrivia" in their lives.

So many of the things we do as adults need to have "miracle cures" to take the tedium away and put in the play. I am waiting for the day when I see someone with headphones grocery shopping. Maybe they will be listening to music. Maybe they will be learning to speak French. But one way or the other, keeping play in their lives.

When you are getting the oil changed in your car, you have time to play! When you are in line at the bank, you have time to play! These things are not a waste of our time, but an opportunity to play in a new way, and change your mood and eventually your life.

16
Color Your Life
With Play

This is the chapter where the rubber meets the road. I am going to talk to you about a methodology that I started using a while ago and have been passing along to my seminar participants over the past year.

The reason I call this system "Color Your Life" is because I feel that play is a colorful thing. I don't think of play as black or white, but blue, green, indigo, orange, yellow and so on. Women are by nature colorful beings. We add the spice of color to rooms, clothes, cars and more. Only in the last few decades have men even worn shirts in pastel colors, and many still rely on the "white shirt" standard.

Since we are so colorful, our lives and our calendars should be the same. Now my methodology here is a little hampered by the advent of the palm pilot. But, do not despair, even the palm can be translated to hard copy and colored and that is what you will need to do.

Now you need to begin to pick the colors that match you and the major things that are in your life. Let's start with the basic colors of blue, green, yellow, orange, and pink, colors that come as a ready-made set of highlighters in most office supply stores. With these highlighters you will begin to see where you spent your time in the past few weeks. Then you are going to plan how you spend your time in the coming weeks, months and hopefully, years.

One of the things that may help you think about colors to describe your life is an understanding of the chakra colors. These are the colors that reference the seven spiritual centers of the body according to yogic philosophy. We will go over these briefly. The first chakra represents your foundation and is symbolized by the color red. Your sensuality is the next point on the spine and is represented by the color orange. Your mid-abdomen is the center of your power and represented by the color yellow. Your heart is represented by the color green. The color blue represents your throat area where you speak your truth. Your wisdom is represented by the color indigo, and finally your connection with spirit is represented by violet. With these chakra colors in mind think about how you would like to color your life, and be free to chose different colors for different reasons.

The first color you need to decide on is the color for your work. If you work outside the home you leave your home at a particular time each day and then return at a certain time. You may even do this several times a day if you have a type of work requiring you to be in many places at different times. If you work in the home you begin your tasks at a particular time and end them at a particular time throughout the day. To pick the color that most suits your work you need to think about what your work is for you. Is it something that you have to do to eat and pay the bills, but you don't really like that much? Is it something that you really like to do, but it takes a lot out of you and you wish it were somewhat easier than it is? (Many people in the "caring" professions find themselves in this category. Nurses, teachers, police people, social workers, even people at the motor vehicle bureau). If your work is total joy and you race to do it every day and feel like you are playing, it is different than just a job. In my old career I would have used green for the color of my work for two reasons. First, I did it from my heart and loved what I did. Second, I associated my work with money, thus the color green. My new work is colored in blue because it involves speaking my truth all the time, which wasn't always easy in my earlier careers. It is still my heart work so maybe I have turquoise as my true work color. A little blue and a little green.

Now you need to pick your chore color. Sorry folks, even in a play book those chores rear their ugly head. Our word for these in the last chapter was, "administrivia." Chores start right when you get out of bed in the morning. Showering, shaving, helping the kids, getting breakfast, feeding animals, watering plants and getting the morning paper out of the driveway all qualify. Going to the dentist, getting your oil changed, picking up groceries and shuttling children or parents also qualify. We have a lot of chores in our lives. Doing dishes, cleaning house, paying bills, taking out the trash, mowing the lawn, sewing on a button, laundry, taking the dog to the vet, taking us to the doctor and on and on and on. Now here is a good time to see how you look at the chores in your life. Are they drudgery to you? Do you put them off? Do you use them as play time and listen to music or dance while you do them? Do you just not think about it and get them done? For some reason I have always used purple to color my chore time. It has nothing to do with chakras or anything other than what color spoke to me when I had to pick a chore color. What is amazing is how many chores I squeeze into a day. Today I answered the phone and a friend asked what I was doing. I replied that I was trying to get lunch, but when I opened the refrigerator I suddenly felt compelled to clean it and an hour later still no lunch, but the refrigerator was clean. Chalk up another hour of purple on my calendar that day or maybe I was playing. Sometimes, sick as it sounds, I get a real kick out of things like cleaning the refrigerator.

One of my favorite colors to pick is my devotional color. This can be described in a variety of ways. If you were a lawyer, it would be called "pro bono" time, meaning "done without compensation, for the public good." (Dictionary.com). This can just be as simple as taking a call from your Mom or a friend when they need you to listen. It can be as complex as building a house for "Habitat For Humanity," or walking to raise money for a worthy cause, or cleaning along a highway or babysitting. You are not paid for it, it is not a chore, and it is done to help someone. For some people this is done in the family. Helping Dad with the yard or Mom with some errands. Maybe the kids raise money for school. Others are actual volunteers with the Red Cross or any worthy cause. Occasionally this color brings up anxiety because people think they don't do anything in this realm and will have nothing to color. Do not fear, you will find more than you know when the time comes to put color to paper. Maybe you do all your devotional work in one big weekend a year. There really are no rules, so don't worry if nothing comes to mind right away. This same color will also be used for spiritual or religious practices during your week. If you attend church, mosque, or temple, prayer meetings and other religious or spiritual observances, this would be the color. Your participation in these things shows the intention of making this a better planet by making yourself a better person, thus falling under the heading of "devotional." Meditation may also be in this category rather than exercise, depending on your perspective and practice.

Your health color is next on the agenda. This is the time we spend exercising, meditating, practicing yoga or tai chi, and anything else we do for the purpose of increasing our health. For some people this is taking vitamins, getting a massage, or soaking in a hot tub. They all qualify if they improve your health either physically or mentally. Your color should represent how you feel about taking care of your health. What do you do to stay healthy? When do you make time for it and how does it affect you? Is your exercise routine, required, programmed? What does your exercise regimen do for your spirit while nurturing your body? Does your body like the exercise you have chosen for it? Does your exercise meet some of the criteria for playfulness?

Now comes your color for rest. This color is often hard to put down because many of the calendars made today will cut off around your bedtime. To emphasize the importance of rest in our lives, pick your color carefully. Even though it will not show up prominently on your daily pages, it carries a great deal of weight in your overall being. I encourage women to write a number in the line they have colored to represent how many hours of sleep they are getting each night. In a seven-day period, that number should total 49 at a minimum. It's a good quick way to check up on another part of your life that is critical to healthy play, how rested you are to enjoy the play. I have been sorely tempted in writing this book to make my rest and play colors the same. My reasoning is that restful sleep is so revitalizing that it feels like play when you wake up.

Well, you knew we were headed this way. The time has come to pick your color for play. If you are playful, you probably picked it out before we started with the other colors. Before you settle on a play color, however, let's look at what you think play is for you. Do you believe real "Heart Play" can change your life? Do you know yourself well enough to conjure up joy from your "Heart Play" right at this very moment? And if so, do you see the color it represents? Choosing your play color can be conflicting between what it has been to us and what we want it to be. As you choose this color close your eyes and see joy. See yourself laughing and smiling. Feel yourself in ecstasy. Now visualize a color. If it is the color you have already chosen for something else, think about that. Think about whether you can create a variation on that color or leave them both the same. An example would be work and play being the same, or exercise and play.

Your play color will be purposefully put on your calendar in the future, and it is important that it "talks" to you.

I have pink for my play color. Pink says to me frivolous, fun, party, frilly, weddings, baby showers, dolls, candy, playful things from childhood and life in general. There was a company in Denver called, "Giggle With The Girls." They had a "Fabulous Pink Party" this past winter and everyone came dressed in pink! I am guessing everyone played and had a good time, too.

Color your life. Wear your play color. Change your colors as your life changes. Find new colors for the new parts of your life. Expand your categories and expand your colors. Life is not black and white. It is a thousand different colors, shades and adventures.

17

"I Just Can't Play"
—Dealing With Resistance

Resistance to play comes in many ways, shapes and forms. Let's start with the resistance to play time that comes naturally to our way of thinking. We don't have the time, the energy or the money to play the way we want. True or false? Time is a killer, that is for sure. The days are short with so much to be put into each of them. If we believe the media, there are a thousand other things we should have gotten done today so how can you even think about playing. Have you researched your children's vaccines on the Internet recently? Been on the home shopping network to buy something? Grown your own organically safe vegetables? Made a trip to the community center to help out? No? Then how can you possibly think about playing!!!!

Where the initial resistance comes in is when you accept this belief that there are so many things that we should do by the media, your family and your well-intentioned friends.

As you start your play journey, you have to think about how you perceive your time and the resistance you feel right now about the non-play things you have to do. We talked earlier about time wasters and miracle cures, but this is more about what you really want to do with the little free time you have found. So often we go through this exercise with women and find that once they have found time to play they find a way to fill it with other work again. I can testify to this because I am a master at it. Find me time to play and I will find more, new or different work to do. Now I want you to know that at this point in the book I know all my friends are laughing their heads off saying, "yep, that's Barbara". Would your friends say similar things about you? Our friends are strong allies on the journey to play, so heed their good feedback.

You have to decide that you are truly committed to the time and energy needed to get into your "Heart Play." Putting play back into your life is no cakewalk. You will have to labor at this, but your work will be a labor of love. You will have to take and make the time to think long and hard about what you want to do. You will make foolish mistakes and be able to stand the ridicule it may bring. You will make many mistakes. You will have false starts. And if you push through all this resistance, you will not only have play, but "Heart Play." Your life will never be the same. It will just get better and better.

Start overcoming this sort of built-in resistance by thinking about what you will say to your life partner, closest friend, mother, sister or dog. What are the words that you will use to describe why you want to do this? What words will convey how important this journey is to you? What words tell about the longing in your heart for something that will soothe your heart? I have heard many people talking about making major changes in their lives. It seems that the thoughts and words that we use to describe our need for change are also used by people trying to explain their need to play. What are your words? What is behind those words? Do you long to feel free like you did as a child? Do you long to be outdoors more? Do you long for more quiet or solitude? Do you long for a piece of your day that is unstructured and an outcome that is irrelevant? Find your words, say them, tape them and write them down. Remember our contract with ourselves that we did earlier? Now it is time to articulate more of the feeling in the commitment.

Our life partners can get very skittish at this new idea to find our "Heart Play." Should this be the case when you begin your journey, I would suggest a few things to put both of you at ease. First, you are going to be a much better person for having "Heart Play" in your life again.

Second, quite often finding your "Heart Play" can bring the partner to find theirs or spend more time with what they have already found. Everyone wins when we play at things we love. Third, you are not suddenly going to leave a sink full of dirty dishes for a month, or stop bathing your children or stop buying food. Remember we are trading nonessential life functions for the time to play, and with our clear thinking from playing more we'll be more effective and efficient at everything we do. Fourth, play makes us more loving wonderful people. One of my favorite quotes is from Diane Ackerman, who says, " Risk stimulates romance and deep play thrives on a romance with life." Now isn't that a great thought?

One way to really get some help with this resistance to play is to engage your children. Depending on their ages you will be met with glee, scorn, or blank stares. I think this is an interesting challenge to us. What do our children know and not know about us? Will they be willing accomplices on our journey or will they be challenges that make us more determined to find our play? Sometimes a foil is as stimulating as a helper. My children look at me and shake their heads, but are also challenged to find their own "Heart Play" when they see how much fun I am having.

I'll always remember asking my Mom on her 60th birthday what it felt like to be "that old." I wasn't exactly tactful. She told me that in her head she was 16. She had a smile on her face that agreed with that statement, and I have already told you how hard she plays. I would like to think my sister, brother and I are willing accomplices to our parents' play. We are challenged to be like them.

The next area of resistance is about keeping promises to yourself. If you say you are going to take Saturday off, will you keep this promise? I have struggled with this all my life as others have. A last minute call, a slight change in the weather, a pile of laundry yet undone—they are all convenient excuses not to keep our promise to ourselves to work on our play. The only solution I can offer here is that if it were someone else, ask yourself if you would keep the promise. Give yourself the gift of keeping promises to you, the **gift of play**. You will find that all those excuses will gradually fade away and it will become easier and easier to stay with your play.

Believe it or not some people have trouble getting into their play because others will make fun of them. No matter how strong or big your ego, I must say that no one wants to be made fun of. If this happens to you how will you deal with it? It is important to look at this area of resistance, because if you are about to go and pull out 200 dolls, put them all over your house and play with them again, you will find that someone is going to make fun of you. If you decide you are going to wear purple hats all the time, someone is going to make fun of you. If you are going to make your own clothes, even if they look great, someone is going to make fun of you. If you decide to breed strange looking dogs, someone will make fun of you. How strongly do you feel about what you are about to do? Are you ready, willing and able to handle any criticism that will come your way? I received some feedback early on in writing this book that it was frivolous, unnecessary and even heard, "why would someone read that?" Fortunately for me I knew whom I was writing for and no amount of negative feedback was going to hinder this journey for me. This is part of my play, I love it and they are welcome to their opinions.

A hard part of playing can be what it may do for us with the people we work with. You have probably been in an office situation where the conversation turns to the "strange" hobby of someone. You may have even seen the distain by a boss when someone needs an extra day off to go to Sturgis for the motorcycle run—that look of "what kind of person is this really?" I think everyone has a right to their privacy so if you do not want to share your play activities you should not have to. Having been in Human Resources for 28 years I know how much managers like to get to know their candidates with the "personal interests" area of questioning to see if the employee will fit in the office. Whatever "fit in" means, it sure is great to know that people like to play golf or softball, particularly if that is an office event. But what if the person says bird watching? Does that immediately label them a nerd? Would you suddenly be perceived as nerdy if you took this up now? You will have to check your resistance to getting into play because it may not look good to those you work for and with. If you are struggling with this you might want to spend some time again asking yourself what is most important. Being authentic through your play, or being what others think is the way to be? I have a strong bias here. Choose YOU.

You can see that these questions are focused on how committed you really are to your play path. They are trying to get you to say that I want to do this so badly that I will be able to explain easily how important this is, and they will see that. My boss will also understand that I will be a much better employee when I have this part of my life fulfilled as well. The question is, can you do it?

Beware of another pitfall in this issue. Passive resistance. Passive resistance comes in the form of "Sure honey, we will do everything we can to support you," then that never happens. This is way too easy for the people around you to do. When you set out your "play plan," set out the rules for everyone else, too. They need to know that you are serious and what you expect in terms of support. After you are in full swing, they will not look back because you will be such a joy to be around!

Do not resist the urge to play at anything that feels like play to you. For example, I am basically not a shopper. Give me a catalogue and I'll get a dress. Send me to a store and I am totally bored. There is one big exception to this. Give me a really good girlfriend in a great big place that has home furnishings and we can spend hours dreaming on how we would like to redo our houses. This is totally "Heart Play" for me. For one, I enjoy the company. Secondly, I enjoy the creative aspect as we put this with that, and laugh at what we would never have in our homes, and wonder who would. We are a lot like little girls in that we are "playing" with a thought or idea that doesn't necessarily need to manifest. Often we do create a new look for our homes. Women like to shop. The misunderstanding may be that we do not all like to shop in the same places. Again, I am one that does not enjoy all the little stores in tourist towns. Not play for me, but heaven for someone else.

Let's finish up all this resistance with "THE EXCUSES." These little monsters are everywhere. In our heads, our hearts, on the lips of others, you will find them without looking too hard. Here is a list. See if you can find one or two of your own on here.

- ✓ I weigh too much now
- ✓ I'm out of shape
- ✓ I've lost the strength
- ✓ There's no one to go with me
- ✓ My voice has changed
- ✓ We sold/gave away all the equipment
- ✓ It takes too much time
- ✓ It's too much trouble (work)
- ✓ My legs, arms, back, head, shoulders, brain, can't take it anymore
- ✓ I've lost my touch

Can you hear all the excuses? Even if any of it were true, it does not mean there still isn't some other way to play at the things you love. Notice how I say play the things you love. If they really weren't your "Heart Play" to begin with, these excuses give a nice out from something you never enjoyed all that much anyway.

Whenever I hear these excuses I cannot help but think of a trip to the ski slopes several years ago. I have always loved skiing, but had allowed myself to get out of shape years before this particular trip. My unresponsiveness and quickly tired muscles made for some scary runs and I lost some of my enthusiasm for skiing. Then, a very good friend took me skiing and made the day as gentle as possible on me. She spent the entire day very patiently showing me why I loved to ski, and that even with more limited abilities I could have a very good time. I realized then that I had choices in my play. I could recondition myself, not a bad idea anyway, or I could recondition my thinking to enjoy the sport at a different pace. Being on the mountains in fresh powder, with breathtaking views and the wind in the trees is something I do not want to miss. Some people even LEARN to ski at age 70. I think I will be okay for a while yet. Melody Beattie in her book *Journey to the Heart* writes about a woman who asks for a wetsuit for her 70th birthday because her arms are too weak to water-ski and she now wants to take up skin diving. We have alternatives, look for them.

I have a little addendum to my ski story. On one of my last ski trips with this great friend, I saw a skier who was blind, a skier who did not have the use of his legs, and a skier with only one leg. It made me take stock once again of what we can overcome, if we really want to.

18
Why So Many Women See Work As Play

Women are very fortunate in that they have always been programmed to follow their hearts. This leads to women quite often ending up in careers that are so joyful to them they are literally playing while they work. Women have a demand in their lives and that is that when they go to work; the work gives them something in return besides a paycheck. What work can give them quite often is the opportunity to "play" at what they do.

Let's talk about some people who are already doing this. You may even be one of them.

Emily began her career after college as a stay-at-home Mom. After the boys were in school she got her Master's Degree and then went on into the workforce as a social worker. Over time Emily became increasingly discontent with her chosen profession. It wasn't fun, only marginally financially rewarding and often very mentally draining. Emily thought about what was really fun for her, and determined that she just loved going into new homes, old homes, looking at homes for sale on line, visiting the Parade of Homes and so on. She studied for her real estate exam and became a realtor. Now she loves her work, and most of the time finds it playful.

Terry was always good at public relations and marketing, but over time grew weary of doing the same thing and decided that she was ready for a bigger and better challenge. This challenge came to her in the opportunity to build a new company based on the best ideas implemented around the country. For several years Terry flew around the country to study innovative facilities. She found the best plans and ideas of others and then put them all together to build a new company. Now she is set to run this company as her next challenge.

These two stories are about people in one career who switched to another to increase their "fun," but what about those who have been having fun all along? You know who these people are, they are the ones who can't wait to get there in the morning, see every challenge as an opportunity to create a solution, and keep things moving along. You and I see these people every day. They can be grocery clerks (do not laugh, I know grocery clerks who love their jobs), bank managers, stockbrokers, teachers, nurses, florists, caterers, sales personnel, and on and on. Any job can be playful for the right person in the right situation. While Emily did not find social work playful for her, I have a cousin who loves her social work position. As we have heard before, "one man's junk is another man's treasure," so it is with work.

This was demonstrated to me in the strangest way several years ago while I was taking a class in Arizona. One part of the week involved not riding horses, but working with them. Up to this point in my life I would never have thought of shoveling horse manure as fun or playful. Not being a "horse person," I was hesitant at best when they told us we would be cleaning the horses as our class one morning. However, during the hours that followed I learned a great deal about these wondrous animals. And while I still don't ride, mucking out a stable would actually be my idea of fun, now and then. Work is very much a mental state, and I hear people talk all the time about how they could never be the one holding the sign on the road work crew. But for some of these people it is a great opportunity to be in the sun all day while composing music or poetry, or writing a book in their heads!

In my great list of jobs I would never want, I had put the job of being the intake person at the Humane Society. Knowing that not all the animals would be adopted, it would break my heart to be sending them on their way. Then I met someone who explained to me what a special job that was to give the animals love and comfort before they passed on. A new perspective, still not my idea of playful or fun, but it could be rewarding to the right person.

You know if your work is play for you when you can answer four simple questions about your job or career. First of all, how do you feel when you are getting ready to go to this work? Happy, joyful, excited, enthused, can't wait to get there, exuberant? Even if you feel a little of any of these, you are probably having a good time at work. Sometimes that isn't due to the work itself but where you work, such as the outdoors, or in any beautiful location. It might be whom you work with that makes it a playful experience, or maybe it is the people you get to meet while you do your work. I can't imagine that the life of a rock star road crewmember is very easy. They drive all night to set up for a show, grab a few winks, tear down the set and get to do it again the next day and the next and the next. But look at the people they get to work with. Look at the places they get to visit. Probably just a little bit of fun there.

Karen works for a Title company. If you have ever bought a house you have met someone in her profession during the closing. Her work is paperwork, deadlines, and changing numbers right up to the last minute. Her work is also seeing the smiles, the hugs and the happy tears as people begin to realize the dream of their home. The work can be tedious and stressful, but it also has an element of play when the deal is done. She has told me that people have brought champagne to their closings, even cameras to take the pictures of everyone involved. Such joy in the midst of such stress comes from the people they get to meet every week.

I mentioned earlier that I knew a grocery clerk who loved his job, so let's look at why. There are three things that Tom loves on this planet; fishing, people and participating in Native American rituals. Tom has a regular stream of customers who come through his checkout to talk "lures" with him. He can work nights to fish mornings, he can switch shifts easily to attend Native American events on the weekend, but most of all he can talk to people all day while checking their groceries. He has figured out how to work and play, and sometimes the lines blur as to which is which.

The next question about work as play is how much are you in control when you are working? I don't mean control in the sense that you can manipulate every situation to your complete satisfaction, but in the sense that you are doing what you know how to do well, and that people let you. Does your work tell the world who you really are? Are you giving of yourself in such a way that your best talents and abilities are utilized, and you are free to be the real you? Look around you and think about the people you have seen today, yesterday, and in the last week who are doing just that.

My hairstylist is one of these people. She works in a salon that allows each person to be an independent contractor in the facility who works, as they want, when they want and how they want. She is delightfully happy in her work, and it shows in her face and behavior. I look forward to my haircuts just to be near this wonderfully happy person. I have also had wait staff personnel where the restaurant owners encourage them to be their own person with the customers and have fun. They have made the dining experience a wonderful adventure for both of us. I enjoy the meal and the banter, they enjoy my good tips.

Another way to look at this would be how free do you feel when you are working? When I work with my clients in finding work in their "Heart Play" I am sensitive to how much they want to be free, and want to risk financially. There may be a need to have their freedom curbed, just a bit, in order to feel more secure financially. Have you made this tradeoff? Are you comfortable with it or is it something to think about? We all know that the first thing out of someone's mouth when you say "Why don't you quit that job and get into something you like" is "I can't afford to."

How does that work for us? I heard someone say once, "If everybody quit the job they didn't like who would drive the cabs, stock the shelves, etc.?" Right after hearing this question I had the opportunity to watch a television special interviewing New York City cab drivers about their jobs. One gentleman, who had been a lawyer in a previous life, was going on and on about how much he loved driving his cab and wouldn't give it up for the world. That's who will drive the cabs if we all do the work we love.

Your next question about your work as play revolves around freedom in another way. This is the freedom of being absolutely who you want to be, truthfully, all the time. What this means is that you are not compromising your principles, your integrity, your values or anything that is part of your core self. Over time I have had the chance to watch this type of compromising play out over and over again in my own life and the lives of people around me. My own story was one of not being true to who I really was and what I believed. As the Vice President of a major company, I truly believed in my heart that work should be fun, that treating people well came along with making money, and that recognizing the contributions of employees should be high on the list of things to do each day, week, month and year. For two years I struggled in an environment where none of these things were valued. Like a pebble on a beach, my feeble efforts to create all these things in the workplace were lost in the "gold rush" of profits. For a while I fooled myself that the work was play for me as I tilted my sword against the windmills, but it was not play for three reasons. First, I was not rushing to work with enthusiasm, I really had no control over my work or the results, and finally, I was not being true to myself and what I believed in.

The last question around work as play is how completely committed are you to what you do? When we get married we make a commitment, when we have children we make a commitment, we even make a commitment when we buy a car. What is our commitment to the work we do? Work is play if we are totally committed.

Emily, our realtor above, is totally committed to her work and her customers, and she is playing all the time because of this commitment. When I have a problem in the grocery store, Tom will move heaven and earth to help me. This is what committed people at work look like. My friend Becky is an interior designer. She is very good at her work and loves it, however she is totally committed to a life of joy. When she gets a client who begins to take this joy from her, she will forgo the income and leave the client. Now that is commitment.

Now leaving our work on principles, or working at something we love that does not feed our children is not reasonable in all cases so let's close this chapter by looking at what we can do with the work we have now that isn't quite the play we would like it to be.

First, pick the most irritating thing about your work and write it down at the top of a sheet of paper. For this exercise we will pick a common one, such as the work is boring, or it's work I've done before is not challenging. Now below this write what you would do instead of this job, if you had the chance. For example, sleep all day, golf, play with my kids, travel, work in a gallery, work for the President of the United States, etc. Play with this for a week or so. List everything you can think of you would rather do instead of this boring job. After the week is up do the same exercise, except this time write down everything you could do to make the job you have now be more fun. Play with this too. Write down things like:

✓ This would be more fun if I had a 360-degree view from my office.
✓ This would be more fun if I worked alone, or with others.
✓ This would be more fun if my boss were someone else.

Keep going for another week until you have converted your current job into a job that is playful and fun.

Now with this second list, after you have really worked on it for a week, start making it happen. You heard me, make it happen. If you wanted a 360-degree view, start collecting pictures of that view and putting them up on your walls. If you want a different boss, start looking at your boss differently. Learn to think about them, as not your boss, but as someone you know and really, really like. Talk to them that way during the week. Smile at them; listen to them closely, even when you don't like what they say. Find out if they have kids, pets, hobbies, find something to like! Keep this exercise going over time. Let yourself "play" with everything that comes up that you do not like and make it into something you can either live with or, better yet, actually like. Life is too short. Work is necessary, so play with it and have fun.

19

The Blessings
of a Playful Life

It is not hard to see how putting play into your life will bring many rewards. In gathering information for this book and talking to many, many women about their lives, it was obvious that those who put play into perspective, gave it some priority and took the time to find their "Heart Play" were reaping the rewards on a daily basis.

One thing I noticed about women who had lost their ability to play and then regained it was their new appreciation for its merits. They would never let themselves get that far away from their play again. To do this they were literally "coloring" their lives each week. Making sure that they had a balance between the work they chose to do, the exercise they needed, and time with friends and family. In so many cases bringing play back into their lives <u>created</u> time with friends and family that had been previously lost.

For example, Terry found herself skiing again even though she had quit after becoming too busy. Her family now surpasses her in skill, but they still go out as a family and she skis different levels than they do. She told me that the solitude of that time in the trees and on the slopes is magical. Meanwhile, she is still with the family for the trip, for lunch and the overnight stay at the resort and have great times together. I have watched several of my friends take up things like Yoga, then find that their daughters, sons and spouses want to join them. The blessing of exercise, play, and family have all rolled into one.

One of the blessings of a playful life may initially appear to be more of a curse. As some women get back into their play they find a discontent brewing with their current lives, jobs and situations. This can manifest itself into a full-blown breakaway from the life they knew. They will leave a job that is stable, steady and sure and find themselves trying to make their play their work. This is not something that they planned to do, and it can be very scary from a financial point of view. But true "Heart Play" can be so compelling that an individual feels the need to at least attempt to make it their livelihood. A friend of mine, Katie, is on this path at this time. She has been fascinated by Art her whole life. She is also someone who believes in giving to the community, especially children. At this time she is in the process of setting up her own studio and teaching Art after being in a very different career for most of her life. Regardless of how her situation develops she is now receiving the blessings of doing something she loves everyday. It is a struggle, and not everything will go perfectly, but what fun she is having along the way.

Another blessing that "Heart Play" brings is confidence that life is good. I have watched women go back to sewing and wearing with pride their beautiful creations. I have watched women take up the rigor of triathlon training and seen them smile with pride at every accomplishment along the way. I have seen women begin to paint again and show their works to others. I have seen women dancing again after years of holding still. When they dance they are at play, their hearts flying along with their feet. All these events have created a new confidence that life is good, that they are good, and that play is a gift that we choose to unwrap.

Sometimes the blessings of a playful life come in a more subtle form. When women who grew up playing as children do not play as adults, discontent pervades their lives until the play returns. And when it does return, suddenly things begin to come into perspective for them. They can see what they want in their work, their marriage, their relationship with their children, and in their friendships. This perspective is a blessing that is found again and again when the playful self is exercised on a regular basis. The freedom and joy that accompanies the playful experience is not unlike meditation or massage, where you are open to the possibilities around you. You find that you see an old friend in a new light and try to reconnect with them. Maybe even inviting them to join in your play. You rediscover the things that were wonderful about that friendship and begin to enjoy not only your "Heart Play" but also the person again. Playing with your children invites the opportunity to communicate with them on a level different from when you are discussing school, chores, or other more routine things. You can be seen by them as playing from your heart, and likewise you see them playing with their hearts. This is a new view, a new perspective that will help when the tougher things in life come up, all brought to you through play.

A playful life has a million other blessings that you will find along your journey. It will sometime challenge you by creating discontent with your current situation. It is going to give you the gift of perspective just when you think you have none. Play will let you get in touch with places in your heart that you have not been to in years. This is painful initially, but eventually it will bring the joy of life as its gift.

You cannot continue to think as you have before, that it is a luxury to play. It is as necessary as food, water, rest, work, family and all the other important ingredients of life. It is important to know what your "Heart Play" is. You cannot ignore this part of your life and expect everything to work out in time. You will have to make a concerted effort to find it, make time for it, and honor it over the length of your life. If you are so inclined you may continuously look for new "Heart Play" to spice up your life. Or, give new time and attention to the same "Heart Play" and expand it into new realms of joy for yourself.

The women of this world who have found and hold dear their "Heart Play," are easily recognized. You will find very little complaint from them about their situations at work, in their families, in their wealth, in their health, or in their relationships. Even though they may not be doing well, they have the underlying peace from the joy of play that helps them to know and understand what is happening and to make the best of it.

Does this sound impossible? You will not know unless you try. You are now invited to join the journey along with many of playful seekers that are out there. In our final chapter we will take you through an exercise that will show you how all of this works, comes together, and will leave you blessed with a playful life.

20
The Eighth Day
of the Week

To really comprehend what a playful life is like, it is necessary to pretend. Just like when we were children, we need to dream, fantasize, and visualize what an ideal playful life might be like. So now come along with me while we completely play for one entire day in a world that is not real, but one that has the ability to tell us what we would like to be and do in our playfulness. This day is not on your calendar. It is not currently scheduled. On this day you are not needed by anyone to do anything. You will not be missed, and nothing can harm those you love while you are gone. They will simply be waiting for you to return.

This day starts out like all fairy tales with "Once upon a time…" Fill in the blanks of this story. Grab a pen or pencil and come along with me while we journey through your own "eighth day of the week." For the purposes of our story we are going to use a woman named Eliza, who does not exist just like the eighth day does not exist. She is going to have a very playful day and show you how to design your playful day along the way. You will need to take your name and substitute it for Eliza's, then you will substitute your own ideas of fun things for what Eliza picked. Or you can do the same things if they appeal to you.

So let's get started.

Once upon a time a woman named Eliza woke up to a very magical and special day. While yesterday had passed on her calendar, today was not there, and tomorrow was not going to happen for another day. After leisurely sleeping in until she was ready to wake up, she arose to a wonderful breakfast of all her favorite breakfast foods. Then she realized that whatever she would like to be or do was hers to have for this day. Because she had thought of this breakfast while lying in bed, it was suddenly waiting for her prepared.

Well, this seemed like an interesting way to live so she immediately went to the next thought that felt good. It was doing some really playful exercise. In her mind this was trying the new cycling and karaoke combination that she had read about, followed by some fun swing dancing where she suddenly knew all the steps and had the partner of her dreams. Soon she was cycling and singing, followed by some fabulous swing dancing with a wonderful partner.

This was getting better by the minute, so she thought she might check out what she looked like. She imagined herself with a brand new hairdo, and an outfit that matched the color of her eyes and made her look ravishing. A quick glance in the mirror showed her imaginations to be real.

This was really getting to be fun.

Eliza now wanted to think about how to spend the rest of her day. She would love to do a million different things. It occurred to her that with her new magical powers she just might be able to do anything she wanted, so she sat and thought. All of a sudden she saw herself playing the piano, although she had never had a lesson in her life. A piano appeared and she sat down and played her favorite songs, perfectly. Next she decided she would play golf. Instantly she was whisked away to one of the most beautiful courses in the world. Her partners were wonderful, fun people and she had a fabulous game.

Now this is the way to live, she thought.

While Eliza was enjoying her day she also missed her family and friends, so she decided to think about some fun things they might do together. In an instant she and several of her best friends were enjoying a wonderful lunch and laughing together. Immediately following the lunch, Eliza was joined by family members for a float trip down a beautiful river surrounded by lush forests, spectacular views and calm blue waters. This time with her family was loving and fun, and they laughed and talked and shared their dreams.

Eliza was really enjoying her day and found herself relaxed and smiling.

Now she thought about a more peaceful type of play. Soon she found herself enmeshed in a pile of big comfortable pillows in a large room overlooking a beautiful valley. Soon she was taken by the serenity of the situation and drifted off into a peaceful meditation. Soft music and tinkling chimes awakened her from this reverie. Her thoughts took her to her body and soon a masseuse appeared and she enjoyed a peaceful massage. This was followed by a wonderful bath with bubbles and rose pedals.

While all this relaxation and play was incredible, Eliza felt something stir inside to be giving, too. Her love of children came to mind and she found herself transported to a preschool setting where she was able to read to a group of inquiring children. Afterwards Eliza found herself out on the playground playing on the slide, swinging on the swings and playing games with the children. She realized that her mind had taken her to that playful space of her own childhood where she was anxious to play that way again. So she got to play with the children.

It crossed her mind how she liked to work with her hands. Instantly she was in a pottery studio throwing pots with others and having the time of her life. She followed this experience with a painting session and then a quick turn through a cooking class.

This day was just getting better and better.

Eliza then thought of her perfect evening. She started out with dinner in Paris, watching the lights come on from a cozy little sidewalk café that brought tears to her eyes. Her dinner partner was the person of her dreams, the one she was the most comfortable with, the one who touched her heart. In the evening she attended a magical theater event, went dancing and capped the evening with a fireworks display over a river.

Truly a playful and heartfelt day.

After a day of this magnitude what more could you want, thought Eliza, but she did want more. She really felt that something was missing in her life, but was having a little trouble putting her finger on it. Eliza sat and thought and thought, but couldn't figure out what was missing. She imagined herself at the top of a mountain meeting with a great guru and sage. This would surely be the way to find what was missing in her eighth day.

As she sat in front of her special guide, she waited anxiously to hear what she had missed. After a period of time her guide looked at her and asked, " Did you follow your heart today?" Eliza said, "of course, everything I thought about came true and it was wonderful." "Then you are missing only your own approval of what you have chosen to do today," replied the guide.

Eliza thought about those words and realized that her guide was absolutely right. It was giving herself permission to enjoy all those things that she had withheld to the end. As she looked back, she realized that she had enjoyed every minute of what was happening because it was a fantasy, and that she would not have given herself permission in real life to do the same.

Eliza went to sleep that night knowing that tomorrow would be a regular day, but that she would find more play and enjoy the moments of play in the things that came her way. She knew she could do many of the things she dreamed about in real life, if she took the time and gave herself permission. Paris might be the French restaurant down the street. The children she read to could be everywhere. The massage can be had for a nominal price with a bit of search and the agreement to give her the time. Eliza had the will and the way to play, she only needed permission.

Let the magic begin.

THE STORY OF BARBARA

Barbara Brannen is a Human Resources Executive with over twenty-five years of experience and playfulness under her belt. She has served as Vice-President and a member of the executive team for such organizations as Qwest Communications, Rose Medical Center, AON/Innovative Services of America and the University of Denver. She is a noted speaker and trainer in the areas of management development, communications, team building, problem solving, and all aspects of Human Resources and Organizational Development.

Barbara is noted for her playful seminars and keynotes such as "Learning To Playmore To Keep From Turning To Toast," "The Gift of Play," "Take Over Your Company and Get Back Your Life," "Problem Solving In The New Millennium" and for leading companies into fun adventures such as her "Unfit Olympics."

Barbara has also created reward and recognition programs such as "The Apple of Your Eye," "Thank You for Bee-ing There," and many more. Her clients enjoy her energy, creativity and always end up having more fun than before she came.

To contact Playmore about Barbara Brannen speaking for your organization or group please call 303-984-9271 or email Barbara@letsplaymore.com. Be sure to visit her website at www.letsplaymore.com.

BIBLIOGRAPHY

Ackerman, Diane. 1999. *Deep Play*. New York: Random House

Beattie, Melody. 1996. *Journey to the Heart*. New York: HarperSanFrancisco

Brigham Deirdre Davis, Adelaide, Davis, and Derry Cameron-Sampey. 1994. *Imagery for Getting Well*. New York: W. W. Norton & Company, Inc.

Clifton, Donald O. and Paula Nelson. 1992. *Soar With Your Strengths*. New York: A Dell Trade Paperback

Cohen, Alan. 1996. *A Deep Breath Of Life*. Carlsbad: Hay House, Inc.

0-595-23426-7

Printed in the United States
202619BV00003B/10-18/A